Books by Martha Bolton

Didn't My Skin Used to Fit?

I Think, Therefore I Have a Headache!

Cooking With Hot Flashes

Growing Your Own Turtleneck

Books by Phil Callaway

Laughing Matters

Who Put My Life on Fast Forward?

Parenting: Don't Try This at Home!

Golfing With the Master

It's Always Darkest Before the Fridge Door Opens

Martha Bolton
and Phil Callaway

BETHANY HOUSE PUBLISHERS

Minneapolis, Minnesota

Published by Bethany House Publishers
11400 Hampshire Avenue South
Bloomington, Minnesota 55438

Bethany House Publishers is a division of
Baker Publishing Group, Grand Rapids, Michigan.

Printed in the United States of America

ISBN-13: 978-0-7642-0307-7
ISBN-10: 0-7642-0307-X

Library of Congress Cataloging-in-Publication Data

Bolton, Martha, 1951-
    It's always darkest before the fridge door opens : finding joy in the cold places of life / Martha Bolton and Phil Callaway.
       p. cm.
    Summary: "Comedy veterans Martha Bolton and Phil Callaway, who believe that God intended for his people to laugh, team up to find the humor in an increasingly trouble-filled world"—Provided by publisher.
    ISBN 978-0-7642-0307-7 (pbk.)
    ISBN 0-7642-0307-X (pbk.)
    1. Conduct of life—Humor. 2. Christian Life—Humor. I. Callaway, Phil, 1961- II. Title.
    PN6231.C6142B65   2006
    813'.54—dc22   2006019510

Dedication

To our loving parents.
We would have settled for money,
but you gave us the gift of laughter.
A million thanks!

About the Authors

MARTHA BOLTON is a full-time comedy writer and the author of more than fifty books, including *Didn't My Skin Used To Fit?* She was a staff writer for Bob Hope for fifteen years and has written for Phyllis Diller, Wayne Newton's USO show, Ann Jillian, Jeff Allen, and many other entertainers. Her writing has appeared in *Reader's Digest, Chicken Soup for the Soul,* and *Brio* magazine. She has received four Angel Awards and an Emmy nomination. She and her husband live in Tennessee.

PHIL CALLAWAY is the award-winning author of fifteen books, including *Laughing Matters, Wonders Never Cease,* and *With God on the Golf Course,* and his articles appear in many publications, including *Leadership, Decision,* and *Marriage Partnership.* A popular speaker for corporations and conferences, he also is a frequent guest on television and radio, including *Focus on the Family.* Phil, his wife, and their three teenagers live in Alberta, Canada.

Contents

Part Four: Empty Shelves (Overworked, Overstressed, Overwhelmed, and Underappreciated—and That's the Good News)

Part Five: Just Desserts (The Best Is Yet to Come)

About the Title

We started talking about writing a book together back when Phil had hair and before Martha was officially banned from kitchens all across America. All we lacked was the right title. We considered titles like *The Whine Driven Life* or *The Elvis on Velvet Code*, but the legal eagles at Bethany House caught wind of these and squashed our hopes. Finally, after at least ten minutes of tax-deductible brainstorming sessions, we decided on *It's Always Darkest Before the Fridge Door Opens*, the book you now hold in your hands. We believe the title works well because:

a. *The Chronicles of Narnia* was already taken.
b. Several publishers offered us contracts.
c. The title made us think of dessert.
d. The title is vague enough for us to insert random humor chapters, then switch to serious things we really believe in, before the reader is fully aware of what is happening.
e. All of the above.

The answer, of course, is *e,* all of the above. We hope that by the time you've finished this book, you'll agree with us that *It's Always Darkest Before the Fridge Door Opens* is the perfect title because, well, it really is darkest before the cheesecake, the leftover pizza, the refrigerator light, and a double scoop of laughter and renewed hope are all staring us in the face. We hope this book is a double scoop of laughter and hope for you.

The Funny Gene

We have both spent a lifetime making people laugh. We have given hundreds of humorous talks and written one-liners for comedians, gags for cartoonists, and text for greeting cards, magazine articles, and newspaper columns. We've even written for politicians. For writing about our quirky views of life, we have both received certificates and awards. We never turn these awards down. We forward them to our high school teachers who told us we'd never amount to anything if we didn't settle down and quit joking around.

Now that we've both hit middle age, many of our parts have indeed settled, and in a southward position, too, but we haven't as yet "settled down." We have found that our humorous take on life has helped us to get through some difficult times, not by laughing at them but by laughing through them.

Laughter has saved our jobs and our marriages, and it has kept us both relatively sane. It has unclogged our arteries and kept us uncommonly thin. . . . Okay, our arteries aren't totally unclogged, but so far the cookie-dough ice cream lining our aortas hasn't broken loose and caused any major damage. Laughter is our life. And it is the only thing left on earth that the government can't tax (though we understand they are working on it).

As much as we both love to laugh, we must confess that there are times we have found ourselves in the "cold places" of life. Swamped by discouragement, trapped beneath our circumstances, robbed of laughter and joy. Maybe you've found yourself in a similar situation. Although we believe that a sense of humor is a gift from God, too many of us seem content to surrender that gift to the joy thieves of life or, worse yet, leave the gift unwrapped, high on a shelf somewhere. Leaving it unwrapped is like undergoing a root canal without anesthesia. You may be able to do it, but boy, is it gonna hurt!

God knew laughter would be important in life. That's why the equipment was installed on the assembly line, but we sometimes choose to ignore it. The emergency brake release button is right there in plain sight, but we bump along neglecting to use it, wondering why we're seeing all that smoke in the rearview mirror, forgetting that we have a built-in release valve that we're not taking advantage of. Surrendering our happiness to bullies or joy thieves is equally self-defeating.

You may be surprised to discover that even comedians don't always live a joy-filled life. As odd as that sounds, many will confess to the truth of that statement. They can stand before audiences of thousands, making them laugh, knowing all the while that their own funny bone is broken and should be in a cast. We both have friends in the comedy world whose lifelong struggle is restoring and maintaining their joy. Before his death, Rodney Dangerfield was asked by *Time* magazine, "Do you think being depressed is an occupational hazard for a comedian?" He answered, "That's the way it is; what can I tell you? The better the comedian, the more depressed he is. When I was 15, I tried to escape being unhappy by writing jokes."[1]

To further prove our point, we could list all the comedians throughout history who were raised in dysfunctional homes, suffered major losses in life, and battled bouts of depression, but then we'd have to sell this book for $240 because of the page count!

In a recent e-mail to Phil, a young father asked the question "Who stole my joy? Please tell me where to find it and how to bring it back."

It is a question both of us hear almost on a daily basis.

---

[1] *Time*, May 17, 2004, 6.

Perhaps you've been asking it, too. Maybe the laughter that once echoed down the hallways of your home is gone. Perhaps the circumstances you are in right now—or have been in for years—have pinned you to the mat. You can't see the sun that rises every morning, much less the fridge light bulb (even though it's there, right behind the brownies). If that sounds like you, then we hope that by the time you've finished reading this book, you'll be on the road to regaining your joy.

Are we saying that your circumstances will miraculously change if you add more humor to your life? No. If you release that emergency brake and laugh a little more, will your estranged spouse come home, will your doctor change that diagnosis that has you consumed with worry, will you have an unlimited supply of money, and will all your children make the dean's list at Harvard? Maybe. Maybe not.[2] Are we saying that the stories and the laughter in the coming pages will help you stress a little less over those areas of life that are beyond your control? We hope so. Can laughter be the lubricant you need when life gets too hard to maneuver through? Absolutely. Will your sense of humor make the pain a little easier to take? You bet. Will a few dozen hearty laughs per day burn up some unwanted calories? Without a doubt, and without even breaking a sweat!

Laughter. The more we learn about it, the more we realize it's nature's wonder drug.

So if, like many of our comedian friends, you buried your funny bone years ago, we invite you to dig down through the pain and disappointment that have covered it all these years, and discover joy and hope once again. We'll even show you some secrets for doing so. And if your sense of humor is in perfect working order and you just picked up this book because you're on a laughter diet and would rather laugh the calories off than skip

---

[2]But if it happens, please let us know.

the carbs, we hope there's plenty here for you, too! Whatever brought you to these pages, we just want you to promise us one thing: If you like even some of what you read here, please feel free to send us a line. We'll forward your note to our high school teachers. It'll make them feel so much better for passing us.

PART ONE

Fridge Magnets

(Bringing Joy Back to Life)

When we lose, I eat. When we win, I eat.
I also eat when we're rained out.
Tommy Lasorda quote, seen on a friend's fridge

Tommy would likely agree that Krispy Kreme donuts are not therapy. They're delicious and may make us feel better temporarily, but eating a box (or two or twenty) of them is not going to change your life or bring you lasting joy. When we go looking for comfort in the fridge, our problems are still going to be exactly where we left them. (What won't be where we left it is our waistline.) But what brings true comfort and lasting joy? Here are some stories and ideas we think will help provide the answer. We also think they will help you laugh.

Warning: If you have a serious addiction to chocolate, please skim this section, as it may give you an unhealthy desire to sell everything you own and drive to Hershey, Pennsylvania.

Chocolate Therapy

Chocolate makes me all better.
Lily Bolton, three years old

Did you ever think, like Forrest Gump, that life is like a box of chocolates, only in your case it seems that someone stole all the best ones and left you with nothing but the nuts? Well, even nuts are a lot more tolerable in almond roca or a strawberry sundae. In other words, there are certain foods that make those rocky, nutty places of life seem to go down a little easier. But we're not sure that anything can help turnips.[1] While some foods are natural energy boosters, and others improve our immune system, others, well, maybe God created to be our comfort foods.

But you may be wondering, just how much comfort is enough? If you start eating chocolate by the fistful before eight o'clock in the morning. to make up for the fact that your husband snored most of the night, is that an allowable amount? The

---

[1]Some foods were not so much meant to be eaten as they were meant to be thrown. Not that we're recommending this.

candy wrapper may have its nutritional facts, but it probably doesn't list any emotional information. It won't tell you how much of it you need to eat for your emotional well-being. Pick up an aspirin bottle and there are warnings and instructions and recommended dosages for removing all kinds of headaches.[2] But how are we supposed to know just how many Kit Kat bars one should eat to experience similar results in our psyches? How many Twix bars are required before we can forget that promotion we know we deserved but didn't get? How big does our banana split need to be to cover that outrageous gas bill? And how many brownies does it take to heal a broken heart?[3] None of these questions can be answered by reading the packages or asking the Baskin-Robbins clerk. Until now, we have had to leave it all to mere guesswork. But thanks to our extensive research team, we're about to change all that. Our Table of Comfort Foods and Cures is not only the first of its kind, it is, we understand, in the running for a Nobel Prize in Science and Home Economics. There is no need to thank us for developing this "feel good" food chart. The research was reward enough.

Table of Comfort Foods and Cures

Crisis	Cure
Kids planning sleepover with four neighbor children	2 cream puffs (lite)
Property taxes due	1 Starbucks mocha Frappuccino, with 1 package of cinnamon rolls
Cable TV out . . . again	6 almond rocas
Fender bender in parking lot	4 Twinkies

---

[2]Yes, there are different kinds. At last count 347.
[3]This was a Bee Gees song.

Fender bender in parking lot at child's soccer game with all the other parents watching	12 Twinkies (remove wrappers before consuming)
Computer crash	3 Snickers bars (2 to eat, 1 to pummel computer with)
Daughter gets driver's license	1-pound cheesecake topped with cherries
Daughter's boyfriend gets driver's license	Eat cheesecake straight from the pan. No fork needed. Forget cherries.
Caught in traffic jam	1 melted candy bar and a hot-sauce packet from Taco Bell, both found under seat
Son brings home report card	2 slices of chocolate cream pie
Teacher comes along when son brings home report card	Entire chocolate cream pie (not to be used for throwing)
Parking ticket	Hot fudge sundae
Parking ticket in front of a Baskin-Robbins	Double hot fudge sundae
Dog bites mailman	7 brownies (3 for you, 4 for mailman)
Mailman bites dog	3 brownies for you, 2 for dog, and a chewstick for the mailman

This, of course, is in no way all-inclusive. There are plenty more examples of food and drink that bring comfort when consumed in the right quantities and at the proper times. But this is something that has been known for years. Certain foods really do bring us comfort. Of course, when we were children and got sick, our mothers had other remedies they wanted to try out on us. Their charts looked more like this:

Illness	Cure
Slight cough	Stay indoors, take 8,000 mg vitamin C every twenty minutes, lots of water, and sip bowl of hot chicken broth (they told us it was chicken, but often it tasted more like soap).
Slight cough worsens	Repeat first cure, then add vitamins A, E, D, H, F, zinc, Old South orange juice, and cod liver oil. (We never understood why they would bother with the vitamins and orange juice since the cod liver oil would usually make us lose them, if you know what we mean.)
Serious, constant cough	Straight to bed with mustard poultice[4] on chest until patient has third-degree burns.
Third-degree burns on chest	Treat area with butter and grated carrots.

---

[4]Half cup mustard powder, 1 cup flour, mix with water. Pancake mix can be substituted, but blueberry pancake mix can cause your doctor to misdiagnose you with a heart problem.

Pain goes away but cough worsens	Apply Vicks VapoRub to singed area. (Provide ear plugs to family and neighbors to block out screams.) Slowly chew four garlic cloves.
Garlic breath	Chew coffee beans and fennel seeds and drink ice water. Or just stay away from people altogether.[5]

I (Phil) don't know about all the other remedies, but I certainly remember how comforting Old South orange juice was to me. When my temperature climbed above one hundred degrees, I loved the joyful sound of my dear mother clanging the wooden spoon (the same one she spanked me with, I believe) around and around in the pitcher, trying to melt that concentrate, and when at last she poured me a tall glass, I knew it was just a matter of time before that fever was history and I would mourn the fact that I had to return to school. (I was shocked in later years to discover that they sell Old South orange juice in grocery stores. I had no idea you could buy it. I always thought Old South came straight from our pastor at the little country church we attended, since he usually arrived about the same time my juice did.)

When we are sick, few things equal the comfort that comes when a friend or clergy member knocks on the door with compassion in his or her heart (and a casserole in each hand). Friends and food make a great pair, don't they? Sitting around the table enjoying six or seven of the four basic food groups all in one dish can be a comfort during the good times and bad.

---

[5]This is a great diet idea and one of the few that really works. Bonus: Without even dieting, you look smaller to people because they stay far away.

In the Bible, the apostle Paul was comforted by friends (Colossians 4:11), contrary to Job's friends, who we don't think even brought a casserole. Paul was also comforted by the love of Christ (Philippians 2:1). What greater comfort could there be than knowing that God loves us; that he will always be with us; that he will never take us where he has not been. The psalmist agrees. "My comfort in my suffering is this," he wrote, "lots and lots of chocolate!" Okay, sorry, that was a typo. No, his comfort wasn't found in chocolate. Or caramel. Or nougat. Or espresso. Or any of the other things that some of us turn to so quickly to find that "feel good" feeling. While some look for comfort at the bottom of a rum bottle or in six pounds of rum-filled truffles, the psalmist found his comfort in God's promises: "Your promise preserves my life" (Psalm 119:50).

May the contents of your fridge be used to comfort others and yourself. But more important, may the contents of God's Word be your eternal comfort.

All praise to the God and Father of our Lord Jesus Christ. He is the source of every mercy and the God who comforts us. He comforts us in all our troubles so that we can comfort others.

2 Corinthians 1:3–4 NLT

You Can't Keep a Good Man (or Woman) Down

There are some things in life that just can't help but put a smile on our face, no matter what kind of a mood we happen to be in. Take, for instance, a Mexican mariachi band. Have you ever tried to stay down while listening to the music in a Mexican restaurant? It's impossible. You may have walked in humming "Nobody Knows the Troubles I've Seen," but after a couple choruses of "La Cucaracha," you'll be donning a sombrero and tapping your flatware to the beat.

Have you ever watched a group of preschoolers sing at a Christmas program while their teachers hover over them, praying against disaster? If you can do so without smiling, you have bigger problems than two humorists can fix.

Here are a few other things it is impossible to do and stay feeling down.

The Hokey Pokey
Be tickled
Eat cotton candy
Wear a clown nose
Juggle[1]
Play with a yo-yo
Yodel
Speak pig Latin[2]
Hold a puppy
Chew bubble gum
Carry a balloon
Swing on a swing set
Ride a carousel
Blow bubbles
Fly a kite
Skip
Listen to banjo music
Ride a stick horse
Listen to a polka
Play the harmonica[3]
Help someone else

A man there was, tho' some did count him mad,
The more he cast away, the more he had.
John Bunyan

---

[1]Unless you're severely down, in which case we wouldn't recommend juggling chainsaws.

[2]Though listening to someone else speak pig Latin may be the ticket to send you over the edge.

[3]Phil once had a Sunday school teacher who played the harmonica professionally and carried a beeper—which was a little optimistic of him.

In Pursuit of Your Passion

Why does SeaWorld have a seafood restaurant?
I'm halfway through my fish burger and I realize . . .
I could be eating a slow learner.

Lynda Montgomery

Some people live to eat. Others live to cook. And some of us (like Phil) live to eat other people's cooking. But even Phil doesn't take it to the extremes that some people do.

At the World Hot Dog Eating Championships held each Fourth of July on Coney Island, New York, Takeru Kobayashi's passion for eating has helped him set the world record. This competitive eater (how come no one offered us that choice on career day at our high schools?) polished off forty-nine hot dogs in just twelve minutes. That's more than one hot dog every fifteen seconds. Though he weighs only 131 pounds, this lean, mean, eating machine has held the hot dog–eating record for five years straight. The reward for eating enough hot dogs to feed a small army? A trophy, a championship belt, and far more important—a year's supply of hot dogs, which at the rate he consumes them, could be enough to feed the Super Bowl attendees.

But Takeru is passionate about the consumption of hot dogs. His nearest opponent was Sonya Thomas, who set the American record by eating thirty-seven hot dogs before the buzzer (and probably her esophagus) sounded.

Nicknamed the Black Widow, Sonya can chow down more in one sitting than a family of eight. Who knows, she might even be able to eat a family of eight if the stakes were right. Sonya is ranked "the number one eater in America." Even more amazing is the fact that she weighs less than one hundred pounds. But she has developed her skill and isn't letting anything get in the way of her goal.

"I am always trying to stretch my stomach," she said in one interview.[1]

How does someone train for eating events like these? According to Sonya, she runs on the treadmill for close to two hours a day and, as a manager of a Burger King, she gets a good workout being on her feet and overseeing the fast-food operation. Sonya also goes to all-you-can-eat buffets whenever she can, which can't help but stretch one's stomach. No one can eat at an all-you-can-eat buffet on a regular basis and not end up with a stomach more stretched out than the national budgets of both America and Canada.

Sonya holds twenty-seven other world eating titles. She has eaten eight pounds, two ounces of fries in ten minutes; devoured eleven pounds of cheesecake in nine minutes;[2] and polished off sixty-five hard-boiled eggs in six minutes, forty seconds. At yet another contest she ate over eight pounds of baked beans in two minutes, forty-seven seconds.[3] But the record she should be most

---

[1] We are, too, but no one gives us a trophy for it.
[2] That one doesn't impress us. We're pretty sure we've done that.
[3] As far as we know, these were separate contests on separate days.

proud of is for oyster consumption. She ate 432 of them in only ten minutes. And was she full at the end of those ten minutes? Amazingly, no. She said she could've eaten even more! This is not someone you could take to a seafood restaurant unless you've just taken a second loan out on your home!

We're sure Takeru trains for his competitions, too. But we can't help wondering why they do it. What drives Takeru and Sonya to train so hard and enter so many food-eating contests? According to Sonya, she does it because she sees competitive eating as an international sport. She would someday like to be treated with the same respect and admiration as sports stars Tiger Woods or Michael Jordan.

Some live to eat, and some live to play. Recently a fifty-four-year-old man was pulled over on a freeway in Toronto. Why? For playing the violin while driving.[4] He told the cops he was on his way to a performance and needed to warm up. He's lucky he didn't play the tuba.

How about you? What is it that you will do almost anything to pursue? What are you passionate about?

Dave Moffitt is passionate about sports. So passionate that for six years he has been living, eating, and sleeping in his Saturn car, driving across America watching sporting events. He has seen every NFL, NHL, MLB, and NBA team play in its home stadium or arena. He has watched hundreds of horse races, car races, golf tournaments, even Little League games. Dave's passion doesn't cost him as much as you'd think. He eats veggies from a can and sneaks hot dog buns into stadiums where he loads them up with free relish, ketchup, and mustard. He shaves in Wal-Mart bathrooms and showers at truck stops. Dave never pays to park, and he finds the cheapest tickets he can. He eats bananas for breakfast and orders lunch from the McDonald's dollar menu. Dave is no

---

[4]This had not yet been addressed in the Vehicle Code.

dummy. He has earned four master's degrees but retired after more than thirty years of teaching junior high phys ed. He just loves sports.

Not surprisingly, Dave has an ex-wife and two estranged daughters. His girlfriend teaches school in Japan, not too far from Takeru Kobayashi's house. As far as we know, Dave's relationship with his girlfriend is going fine, but should she tire of his passionate pursuit of sports, Dave says that they won't be together anymore.

Contrast these passions with the passions of those who are living for something that will outlast them. Mother Teresa was passionate about helping others, so much so that she dedicated her life to serving the poorest of the poor in Calcutta. Billy Graham's passion was spreading the simple truth of the Gospel to as many people around the world as he possibly could. Did he fulfill his passion? We think the answer is pretty obvious.

Someone has defined failure as succeeding at something that doesn't really matter. We hope you're passionate about something that matters. Hopefully your passion won't cost you your relationships, your job, your family, or your digestive tract, but throughout history, passion is what has driven people to great things. A lack of passion equals a lack of joy. Without passion, we're all doomed to a life of mediocrity.

And what are we passionate about?

We're passionate about chocolate, but we're more passionate about reminding people of the importance of finding the laughter in life. I (Martha) am passionate about telling others how much God loves us and has a plan for our lives. I (Phil) have told people that the words I want written on my tombstone are these: "He found God's grace too amazing to keep to himself."[5] I'd like to spend whatever days I have left telling others of God's amazing

---

[5]It sure beats, "See, I told you I was sick," or "Here lies an atheist, all dressed up and no place to go."

and amusing grace, reminding them of our reasons to rejoice, helping them bring joy to life.

And we both love to eat hot dogs at baseball games . . . one at a time.

> Yet if we celebrate, let it be
> that he has invaded our lives with purpose.
> *Luci Shaw*

Fresh Veggies

That day is lost on which one has not laughed.
French Proverb

There's nothing quite like fresh vegetables from your garden to fill a refrigerator's shelves. Fresh corn, fresh radishes, fresh cucumbers, and fresh tomatoes.

There's an old joke that deserves retelling here, since it's about an elderly Italian gentleman who planted a fresh tomato garden every spring. This particular spring, though, he wouldn't have his son, Vincent, to help him dig up the ground, as Vincent was in prison. The ground was rock hard, too hard for the old man to work, so he wrote a letter to his son complaining about his predicament. It read,

> *Dear Vincent,*
>
> *I guess I won't be planting a tomato garden this year. I'm getting too old to be doing all that gardening. If only you were here to dig up the plot, I could do it. But I guess that's impossible.*
>
> *Love, Dad*

A few days later he received this reply from his thoughtful son:

Dear Dad,

> *Don't dig up that garden. That's where I buried the bodies.*
>
> *Love, Vinnie*

At four o'clock the following morning, FBI agents and the local sheriff's department arrived at the old man's house and immediately started digging up the entire area. But to their disappointment and frustration, they didn't uncover a single body. They apologized to the old man and then got into their cars and left.

A few days later the old man received another letter from his son.

Dear Dad,

> *Go ahead and plant the tomatoes now. That was the best I could do under the circumstances.*
>
> *Love, Vinnie*

We tried and tried to think of a great spiritual application for this joke. We called theologians; a few had PhDs. They laughed at the joke but shook their heads when it came to a life lesson. Maybe the application is this: Sometimes we need to quit looking for applications and just enjoy a good laugh.

I felt his presence when you laughed just now.

Phil Keaggy

Eat Like You Were Dyin'

With apologies to the writers of "Live Like You Were Dyin'" (one of the greatest country songs ever written).

Song for a Cruise Ship
　　　　　　　　　　She said, "We were in our early fifties
With a few good years before us,
So let's take this cruise while we've still got the time."
We spent most of those nine days
Standing over food trays,
Scarfing down those scallops
and cheesecake and key lime!
My stomach was a'achin'
and I was leaning on the railin'.
Then it hit me that I ate my weight in shrimp.
So what'd I do?

I went and had another fritter,
I ate Rocky Mountain oysters,
I spent 2.7 hours eating food off that buffet.
And I got sicker and I turned greener,
then I ordered Pepto Bismol and said I'm buying!
And I told them all I'm glad I got the chance
to eat like I was dyin'.

I quit counting carbohydrates
that most the time I hadn't,
and I ordered up a sausage double cheese.
By then I needed a physician.
But I'd give up my position
in the buffet line at midnight every night.
So I ordered up a latte
and I savored one last brownie.
And if I could, I'd sure do it all again!

Because I love those deep-fried pork chops,
and those steaks that keep on coming,
and spending 2.7 hours picking salmon off those bones.
But the boat sank deeper as I got bigger,
still it feels good eating all I'd been denying
and my friend, someday I hope you get the chance
to eat like you were dyin'!

Dinner's Done, Call 9-1-1

*When women are depressed, they either eat or go shopping.
Men invade another country. It's a whole
different way of thinking.*

Elaine Boosler

I (Phil) have pictures on my fridge. Pictures of friends and family
and animals and one of my dad falling off a chair laughing. There
are magnets, too. Imitation cabbages, cauliflowers, bittermelons,
and pumpkins—all fitting the decor of the kitchen. The dieter's
favorite Bible verse is there: "He must increase but I must
decrease." Here are a few of my favorite fridge magnets:

⊚ You'll eat it. You'll eat it and like it.
⊚ Make yourself at home: Clean my kitchen.
⊚ Coffee isn't helping, get the jumper cables.

I (Martha) have signs in my kitchen, too. I have a custom-
made sign that my kids got me for above my stove that says,
"Martha's Burn Center." Other original signs of mine say,

"Dinner's Done! Call 9-1-1!" and "Rolaids—They're Not Just for Breakfast Anymore."

We don't know about you, but we both love the kitchen. It is the heart of the house, the pulse of a family. So much happens in the kitchen. Botulism and putting out fires is only part of it.

First, the refrigerator is there. Need we say more? Nothing brings a family together quite like a weekly game of Guess What It Was. Whether it's a cucumber that now looks more like a Chia Pet, cheese that now weighs two pounds more than it did when you bought it, or the three-week-old pot roast that is now providing a sort of neon lighting for you to see the rest of the food, playing Guess What It Was is a fun and educational game that has been bringing families together since the invention of the refrigerator.

Then there's the stove. How many families have gathered around a skillet engulfed in flames, trying to put out the fire before the neighbors see the smoke and call the fire department again? Nothing bonds a family quite like standing around a roaring grease fire on a cold winter's day.

There's the counter space, too. When I (Phil) built our house, my wife and I had a few extra feet of kitchen counter added so all five of us could make sandwiches simultaneously. This saves time in the morning and puts me close enough to sneak an extra slice of turkey meat off my wife's sandwich when she's not looking.

And finally there's the table. It may provide comfortable seating, or the chairs may be crammed in so tightly, no one can leave the dinner table early even if they were excused. How many family discussions, announcements, debates, arguments ("He's looking at me!" "Am not!" "Are too!"), overeating, and even napping have taken place around the dinner table? It's the gathering place to beat all gathering places.

Whether it's breakfast, lunch, brunch, dinner, or a Thanksgiving or Christmas feast, being together in the kitchen is about as good as it gets. Few things can silence teenagers more quickly than food. And few things can bring a family together faster than a feast. And we haven't even mentioned all the fun food fights yet.

I (Martha) have another sign on my fridge: "Home is Where the Heartburn Is." I was referring to my cooking when I wrote that, but sadly there is a lot of heartburn going on in families today because of stress. We've discovered that one of the leading joy-killers is stress. Our homes can be the most stress-filled places on earth, as we dash to appointments, grabbing half-made sandwiches or half-baked muffins with scarcely a nod left over for one another. In the midst of busy times, here are three items to place on your menu, three suggestions to help you de-stress your kitchen and bring back the joy.

Pray together. There are five more items on my (Phil's) fridge, more precious than any fridge magnets. They are photos of our adopted children, the children we sponsor with the wonderful organization Compassion. Their names are Carlos, Joel, Dariani, Habtamua, and Ndagirijwe.[1] We try to pray for them before every meal. Each of these five lives in a country where food is scarce. Praying for those who are less fortunate helps us remember how much we have to be grateful for, and it is a definite cure for complaints about the leftover tuna salad.

Linger longer. One of the best ways to keep your children or guests at the table longer is to fill their mouths with things they can't resist.[2] And nothing works better than dessert. Time spent over dessert or hot tea and coffee is invaluable in building relationships, and you can make it work for just about any age group. So whenever possible, have dessert. Stop after six helpings.

Ignore the dishwasher. Few inventions (besides the remote control) have pleased us more than the dishwasher, but recently

---

[1] Thankfully, you don't have to know how to pronounce someone's name in order to love them.

[2] Things like your Grandma's fruitcake that are so heavy to digest they can't get up for a while.

in the Callaway house something strange began to happen. Our water got weird on us. The glasses came out murky at best, caked in white. We called the experts, who told us it had something to do with the water treatment plant, and they were working on it. In the meantime we began washing dishes by hand. Our children hardly knew this could be done. But a strange thing began to happen. We started talking while doing dishes. Actually communicating. Do you remember what that used to be like? I taught my daughter the fine art of snapping towels on her brothers' hindquarters. I taught her how to run really fast down the hall and lock the bathroom door behind her, before he could retaliate. We hadn't heard this much laughing and screaming since the time my dad fell out of that chair laughing.

One of the surest ways to bring back the joy is to center on building healthy relationships. And one of the surest signs of a healthy family is the joy and peace and noise and laughter found in the heart of the house: the kitchen.

We are living in a world today where lemonade is made from artificial flavors and furniture polish is made from real lemons.
Alfred E. Newman

Laughing Matters

The most wasted of all days is
that on which one has not laughed.

Nicolas-Sebastien Chamfort

We received a letter the other day from a lady we shall call Priscilla, because that is her name. She writes,

My home is full of tension and absent of laughter. I've wanted to move to a funnier house, but I think the problem is within me. Could you tell me what you find to laugh about? My husband likes blonde jokes and other juvenile humor and, like many boys his age (he's forty-two), he thinks gas is funny. I don't understand his sense of humor, though I will laugh hysterically whenever he does something and ends up injured. Other than that, we don't laugh at all. What would you recommend?

We decided to surprise Priscilla with a phone call. This is a portion of the transcript. (We could only write so fast):

Priscilla: Hello?

Phil: I understand you haven't laughed in a while.

Priscilla: Who's this?

Phil: Phil. Phil Callaway.

Martha: And Martha Bolton. You wrote to us?

Priscilla: Are you Aunt Bessie's kids?

Phil: No. We're writers.

Priscilla: In the rodeo?

Martha: Writers. Not riders.

Phil: So, is it true, you're having a hard time laughing?

Priscilla: I haven't laughed since 1974.

Phil: That's a long time to go without laughter.

Martha: What happened in 1974?

Priscilla: Someone asked me if I knew why the chicken crossed the road.

Phil: And what'd you say?

Priscilla: I'm still thinking.

Phil: Maybe you can find some humor in your work. What do you do?

Priscilla: I'm a mortician.

Martha: Not a lot of laughs there.

Priscilla: It's impossible, isn't it? I'm a hopeless case.

Phil: First of all, you need to understand that laughter is a physiological response to humor. Laughter modifies neuroendocrine components experienced during stress. Psychoneuroimmunology explores the links between laughter and the immune system, and it is now discovering that mirth may actually attenuate levels of epinephrine and cortisol!

Priscilla: Say what?

Martha: What he's trying to say is that laughter is better than bran flakes.

Phil: Solomon knew that thousands of years ago.

Priscilla: They had bran flakes back then?

Martha: Did you know that during a laugh, fifteen facial muscles contract?

Priscilla: I didn't know that.

Phil: And a hearty laugh burns up thirty-five calories?

Priscilla: That sounds great. But where can I find good things to laugh about? I've tried comedy clubs. They can be crude. And there's usually a cover charge.

Phil: Find the funny in the ordinary. Hang out with people who like to laugh. Start noticing the things kids say and the things dogs do. Watch funny movies.

Martha: The biggest enemy of joy is worry. Those who can't laugh are usually filled with fear and anxiety.

Phil: Give your problems to God on a moment-by-moment basis.

Priscilla: Okay, I'll try that. Is there anything else I can do?

Phil: Think of your fridge.

Priscilla: Huh?

Phil: When you put moldy cheese into your fridge and leave it there for three weeks, it won't come out new and improved. Trust me, I've tried it. It's the same thing with our minds. Feed your mind on positive thoughts. Read the book of Philippians in the Bible. Dwell on things that are true and honorable and pure and lovely, and the outcome will be surprising.

Priscilla: And that'll help get my sense of humor back?

Martha: We guarantee it.

Phil: Do these three things and it will make all the difference. Look inside, and let go. Look around you, and get involved. Then look up, and rejoice.

Martha: Just don't look up as you're stepping over an open manhole.

Phil: We hope this has been a help, Priscilla.

Priscilla: I think it has.

Phil: We called collect, you know.

Priscilla: Of course.

Phil: That's how we keep from worrying over phone bills and losing our joy. We call everyone we know collect.

Martha: And it works. We guarantee it!

Phil: Now put your husband on the line; we'll see what we can do for him.

Magnetic Joy

We've already told you that we love fridge magnets. Magnets help draw two surfaces together. And magnetic joy can draw people together. Surely one of the most powerful magnets in our relationships is joy. In Psalm 126:2 we are told what happened when God freed the captives. "Our mouths were filled with laughter, our tongues with songs of joy. Then it was said among the nations, 'The Lord has done great things for them.'" We hope you'll experience a little of that joy in your life. Better yet, we hope you'll spread it around.

**The kind of humor I like is the kind that makes me laugh
for five seconds and think for ten minutes.**
William Davis

The Funny-Bone Quiz

Never eat more than you can lift.
Miss Piggy

Many of us take the time to routinely check our automobiles to make sure various parts haven't fallen off without our noticing them. Many of us get a complete physical on our bodies every year to make sure of the same thing. We do everything we can to keep up with the maintenance on our homes, our computers, our lawns, and our bodies. But do we ever think twice about what kind of condition our sense of humor might be in? Do we take the time necessary to make sure our laughter equipment is in good working order?

To figure out your FBQ (Funny Bone Quotient) and to make sure it is in prime working order, please answer the following questions to the best of your ability:

1. One morning on your way to work, you slip and fall on an icy sidewalk.[1] Do you:

---

[1]If you live in Hawaii, you slip and fall in the hot sand.

a. Use words that would take a whole bar of Ivory soap to wash out.

b. Sue the city, all its employees, the employees' relatives, and anyone who saw you wipe out.

c. Tell the three teenage girls who are laughing at you that you meant to fall; it felt good, and it's part of your exercise program, and you just might do it again because it was so much fun.

2. Which of the following statements best describes you:

a. I believe laughter should be used for medicinal purposes only.

b. When I hear others laughing, I want to put fiberglass insulation in their pajamas.

c. When I hear laughter, I want to know what's causing it, and I will find a way to join in.

3. The server accidentally spills a drink on you while you are eating at a restaurant. Do you:

a. Demand to see the manager at once.

b. Pelt the server with ketchup and sugar packages.

c. Do your best to laugh it off.

4. Your car unexpectedly did a 180-degree turn on a snowy highway and came to rest in the ditch. Everyone is fine, but your pride is wounded. Do you:

a. Scream loudly for thirty seconds (it's your way of gaining your composure).

b. Call the snowplow guy and demand an apology.

c. Change careers and become a stuntman.

5. A driver's impatient horn blast startles you while you are in the middle of a crosswalk. You:

a. *Talk to him with hand signals.*

b. *Kick his bumper and dent his grill.*

c. *Fake a heart attack and collapse in front of his car. Then laugh and walk away.*

6. You just ran across a crowded restaurant to hug an old friend, only to discover it wasn't your old friend. You:

a. *Run to the washroom and cry over the embarrassment of it all.*

b. *Insist that you are an old friend and that they are probably senile.*

c. *Say, "I was just kidding. Now, may I take your order?"*

7. You are awakened from a deep sleep by a phone call. It's an old friend passing through town who has decided to say hello. You:

a. *Say, "You have reached my answering machine, please leave a message."*

b. *Blow a shrill whistle into the phone.*

c. *Ask if they are on Zimbabwe National Time and laugh heartily together.*

8. You have been asleep in the backseat while your spouse drives through the night. Your spouse stops to use a rest room at a truck stop. You wake up and decide to, as well. When you return the car is gone. Your spouse is now five miles away, keeping the radio on low so as not to wake you, thinking you are still sound asleep in the back. You will:

a. *Conspire, collude, contrive, and cook up all sorts of retaliatory things to do to your dearly beloved.*

b. *Tell anyone who will listen how terrible it is to be you.*

    c. *Tell the gas station clerk to expect a call, pray your spouse didn't do it on purpose, and wash windshields while you wait.*

9. Your flight has been delayed two hours. You:

    a. *Let everyone at the gate know how unimpressed you are.*
    b. *Fuss, fume, gripe, moan, mutter, and bellyache. With a side order of carp, grouse, stew, beef, and whine.*
    c. *Won't be thrilled, but what can you do? So you call a friend in the area, read a good book, or spread some cheer. Looks like these people could use it.*

10. When people look at the way I live my life, they are learning . . .

    a. *Not to trust others. Everyone's a suspect.*
    b. *That the fruit of the Spirit is frown, scowl, grimace, glower, sulk, and wince.*
    c. *That those who laugh lots grow old with all their wrinkles in the right places.*

> Mix a little foolishness with your serious plans:
> it's lovely to be silly at the right moment.
> *Horace*

PART TWO

Smelly Cheese

(I Could Cope With the World If It Wasn't for the People)

> I like long walks, especially when
> they are taken by people who annoy me.
> *Fred Allen*

People are like food. If left to their own devices, they can get a little rotten. We've met a few who fit this description, and we imagine you have, too. According to the experts, people are the leading cause of people problems. And according to us, people problems can play a leading role in keeping us stuck in the cold places of life. We will refrain from naming names in this section, because we've been at fault, too. As difficult as it is for us to admit, sometimes the problem lies within us. Oh, we may not be 100 percent at fault. Maybe it's more like 50–50. Or 70–30. Or 90–10. Whether we bear any blame or not, the simple truth is that there are people in this world who love to raid other people's refrigerators and steal their joy. Maybe it's because theirs is so empty. Whatever the reason behind their actions, you still have to know how to deal with them. If one of the best gifts you can give yourself is a friend, here's a little advice (and a bit of humor) on keeping your friendships intact and making peace—as much as possible—with your enemies.

Cold As Ice

Therapy is expensive, popping bubble wrap is cheap.
Anonymous

Ever wonder what the world would be like if the only people living in it were you, those family members you enjoy, and your closest friends? Maybe you'd even allow some people from your work or church, and a few nice people in your neighborhood, to reside here, too—if they behaved themselves and lived by your rules. Wouldn't that be great? Everyone in the world would be people you like. That is, until the first disagreement. Then one half would side with someone else, and the better half would side with you, and before you knew it, you'd be wishing the only people left on earth were the ones on your side. Then that half would have a disagreement and split again, and you'd be wishing the only people left in the world would be your half of the original half. Then they'd divide again. And again. And again, until you'd be the last one left, and by that point, you may not even agree with yourself! Reminds us of the familiar story of the man marooned on a desert island all alone for twenty years. When his rescuers finally found him, they noticed three buildings and asked what they were. The marooned man explained that the first was his house. The second was his church. "What's that third one way back there?" someone asked. "Oh," he replied, "that's the church I used to go to."

Like it or not, the world is made up of people. Wonderful, flawed, pushy, passive, irritating, friendly, difficult, congenial, discouraging, uplifting, selfish, generous, mistake-prone people. And sometimes, we're all a little bit of all of that. We're sometimes clueless, sometimes brilliant, sometimes hurtful, sometimes caring, sometimes giving, sometimes taking, sometimes vengeful, and sometimes forgiving.

We can't get away from the simple fact that we are imperfect creatures in an imperfect world. And if we think we don't have flaws, there are plenty of people in our lives who would be more than happy to point those flaws out to us.

Sometimes, though, when we're trying our best to live at peace with those around us, we encounter those who seem to be working just as hard to rob us of our happiness. These joy thieves buried their sense of humor years ago, and they're not content until they've buried whatever shred of joy they find in the lives of others. From short-tempered sales clerks to annoying drivers to just plain mean, nasty, and spiteful people, we have all had to face these creatures throughout our day, and the encounter is never easy. That's why we decided to include a little advice on how to deal with the bullies, the incompetent, the irritating, the frustrating, the unfriendly, the unforgiving, the difficult, the self-righteous, and perhaps even an enemy or two.

> I didn't attend the funeral,
> but I sent a nice letter saying I approved of it.
> *Mark Twain*

Is This the Party to Whom I'm Speaking?

Forgive your enemies, but never forget their names.
John F. Kennedy

We can't talk about difficult people and not mention telemarketers. Sometimes a polite "no thank you" and a click is sufficient, but dealing with an aggressive telemarketer is like trying to shut off a fire hose with clothespins. Getting your phone number put on the Do Not Call list will help some, but one can still slip through the cracks from time to time—just when you're about to step into the shower. That's why we feel it's necessary to provide you with some handy responses for the next time one of these life intruders calls.

Top Ten Responses to a Telemarketer

1. *"Here, talk to my two-year-old."*
2. *"You'd like to speak with my husband? He died in a unicycle accident just this morning. He collided with an oncoming bear*

in a tutu. It's a risk of circus life. I'm so glad you called. I
have no one else to talk to about it . . ."

3. "Magazine subscriptions? I'll take them all! But first, I have
something I want to sell you, too! Have you heard of
Amway?"

4. "Harry! Is that you? I can't believe it! Marge, come in here
quick, it's Harry! See, I told you he was alive!"

5. "Are you from the dating service? Me and my four kids are
free Saturday and we'd love to go to Disneyland!"

6. "Is this about the money you owe me?"

7. "Grandma! It's for you, and don't talk for two hours like you
did last time."

8. "Telephone solicitors' fraud department. Can I help you?"

9. "Kids! Daddy's back! Come say hi!"

10. "I'm going to have to put you on hold . . ." (Then go on vacation.)

Never explain—your friends do not need it
and your enemies will not believe you anyway.
Elbert Hubbard

The Trouble With Pharisees

*I wanted to do something nice, so I bought
my mother-in-law a chair. Now they won't let me plug it in.*

Henny Youngman

If you've ever stepped foot inside a church,[1] (and we hope you have), you've no doubt heard the song "Amazing Grace." Written around 1772, it is very likely the world's most beloved hymn. I (Phil) heard the Eagles play an instrumental version of it once before seventeen thousand people, and most of the seventeen thousand were singing along.[2] Sometimes you run into people, however, who want to give the song a rewrite. They want to sing, "Selective Grace how sweet the sound that won't save a wretch like that guy." Jesus ran into them, too. They were called Pharisees.

Pharisees point to the wrong. Jesus points to the redemption. Pharisees remind others of their sins while overlooking their

---

[1]And taken the rest of your body with you.

[2]At least, those who weren't sitting near the speakers and still had their hearing.

own. Jesus forgives and erases all sins that are repented of, then remembers them no more. It's not divine amnesia; it's his choice. He loves us so much that he doesn't even know what we're talking about if we bring those sins up again. As Corrie ten Boom said, "God throws our sins into the deepest sea and puts up a sign: 'No Fishing!'"

Sadly, Pharisees are those who go fishing for other people's sins while playing catch-and-release with their own. When an angry mob was about to stone an adulteress who was caught in the very act, what did Jesus do? Condemn her? No. He bent down and began writing words in the sand, words that convicted the hearts of those holding the stones. Perhaps the words were *pride, greed, lying, bearing false witness, coveting, taking the Lord's name in vain, hatred, bitterness, jealousy, fornication, unforgiveness, self-righteousness, self-centeredness,* or any number of other sins. There might have even been a few other adulterers there in the crowd, rock in hand, ready to pitch it at the accused. We're not sure what the exact words were that Jesus wrote, but those words certainly brought conviction to their hearts. Maybe he was more specific. Maybe he started writing their names and then listed their failures. If he got that specific, it wouldn't have taken long for the rest of the crowd to start dropping their stones and leaving the scene before he got to them.

Then Jesus said, "He that is without sin cast the first stone." Wouldn't you like to have been in the crowd, watching their faces? Jesus' words, both the spoken ones and the ones written in sand, must have pricked some pretty self-righteous consciences, because soon the woman was standing all alone. We would have walked away, too, because his mercy holds a mirror to our lives. In this mirror we see our own selfishness. His grace forces us to see our own need for grace. And it's not always a pretty picture.

Aren't you glad that the gospel isn't about selective grace? It's about *amazing* grace. And that grace is available to each one of us, not just those pointing their fingers at others. Whether the rock throwers want to hear it or not, it's true. God's grace is amazing. And it's for each one of us, no matter how small and insignificant our own sins look in our eyes. According to the Law, we're all worthy of a stoning. God offers us what we don't deserve: mercy and grace.

> The weak can never forgive.
> Forgiveness is the attribute of the strong.
> *Mohandas Karamchand Gandhi*

> It is not the critic who counts, not the man who points out how the strong man stumbled, or where the doer of deeds could have done better. The credit belongs to the man who is actually in the arena, whose face is marred by dust and sweat and blood, who strives valiantly, who errs and comes up short again and again, who knows the great enthusiasms, the great devotions, and spends himself in a worthy cause, who at best knows achievement and who at the worst if he fails at least fails while daring greatly so that his place shall never be with those cold and timid souls who know neither victory nor defeat.
> *Theodore Roosevelt*

Enemies:
What Would We Do Without Them?

We must develop and maintain the capacity to forgive.
He who is devoid of the power to forgive is devoid
of the power to love. There is some good in the
worst of us and some evil in the best of us.
Martin Luther King Jr.

Do you have any enemies? People who are like food allergies, and every time you get close to them you break out in hives? People you can't really tar and feather but sometimes find yourself wondering what they would look like stuck in the gooey mess? We're not talking about the occasional rude clerk who won't bag your groceries or that driver who cut you off on the freeway this morning while talking on her cell phone and curling her hair. We're talking about a real enemy. Someone who seems to celebrate when something goes wrong in your life. People who would like nothing more than to see you fail, because it makes them feel better about themselves or their own shortcomings.

If it's any consolation, most people who have ever tried to do any good in life will have had an enemy. Some, like many of the prophets in the Bible, end up having a whole army of them. Sometimes, as was the case with brothers Cain and Abel, the enemy is a family member. Cain was jealous that God had been pleased with his brother's sacrifice and not with his. He could have examined the reasons God was displeased with him and repented, but instead he decided to kill his brother.

By the time Joseph came along some years later, jealousy still had not gone out of style. Joseph's brothers were envious because Joseph was Daddy's favorite, so they plotted to kill him but then decided to make a little cash instead by selling him into slavery. King Saul was jealous of David, choosing animosity over friendship, even though David tried his hardest to be friends. David's own son Absalom staged a mutiny against his father with tragic results. And the list goes on. Throughout the Bible, there are plenty of accounts of good people who, sometimes for no apparent reason at all, other than the fact that they were doing good and making a difference, had to deal with enemies.

But instead of letting an enemy get the best of you, save "the best of you" for those who appreciate it, and give an enemy what he or she clearly doesn't deserve but has a shortage of in his or her life—God's love and grace.

Love is the only force capable of
transforming an enemy into a friend.
Martin Luther King Jr.

"Blessing" Those Who Curse You

The trouble with her is that she lacks the power of conversation but not the power of speech.

George Bernard Shaw

It was Jesus who told us to "bless those who curse you." On the surface, it seems impossible. But you can do it. The key is to be just a little creative. Remember the czar's blessing that was given in *Fiddler on the Roof?* "God bless the czar . . . and keep him . . . very far away." Here are some other "blessings" that we hope will make you smile before we try our best to get serious again:

May your children be blessed with musical giftedness. On the drums, tuba, and bagpipes.

May your mailbox be filled with weekly greetings. From the tax service.

May your children arise and call you. Collect.

May your stereo play CDs loud and clear. But only ones by Barry Manilow.

May you receive news of a large inheritance. May it be a peacock farm.

May you and your spouse receive two letters of good news on the same day: a letter notifying you that your social security retirement benefits will begin immediately and another letting you know your pregnancy test was positive.

May your neighbors on each side of your new house share your enthusiasm for Harleys. May they be in opposing gangs.

May you develop an unwholesome obsession for eating garlic by the fistful.

May your child be a novelist. And write about you.

Come on, admit it, it was fun thinking about these things for a moment, wasn't it? But we both know that these aren't the kinds of blessings Jesus was referring to. In fact, his command "Love your enemies, do good to those who hate you" (Luke 6:27) may be one of the most difficult commandments in history. What? Love my enemies? Surely you're kidding. But Jesus wasn't. His death was proof. He forgave them. His words are liberating. Following his commands is not always easiest, but it is always best.

Thankfully, most of us don't have a long list of enemies or people who love to hate us. But if we're looking for those who irritate us, we won't have to look far.

Right now I (Phil) am seated at gate C-37 of an airport waiting for a delayed flight. A lady five seats away from me is talking loudly into her cell phone. She is telling her child, who must be studying for an exam (and the forty-seven others seated at this gate), the meaning of words like *blurt, fatigued,* and *ambidextrous.*

59

I would like to blurt something about the meaning of the word rude, but I am fatigued. And the more fatigued I grow, the more I am aware of how easily I am irritated these days. My list is long and irritating, but here are just a few of the things that are really starting to annoy me:

I am tired of people who use their luggage to take up three seats at the gate in airports.

I am tired of people who leave grocery carts in parking stalls or straddle the yellow line when they park.

I am tired of children who leave their science project until ten o'clock the night before the Science Fair and expect me to have enough household supplies to help them make something clever.

When I finally make it onto the plane, guess who is seated next to me? You're right. The cell phone walking-dictionary lady. To make matters worse, she is traveling with a cat, and the cat's name is Sweetie. He is in a little kennel at her feet, and he is not happy about it. The stewardess arrives and, bending down, informs Mrs. Dictionary of two rules. First of all, she says, "Do not take the cat out of the bag for any reason." This is good. I'm all for this rule. The second is way funnier. "There is an extra oxygen mask on this row," says the stewardess. I couldn't believe it. The extra mask is for the cat![1] "In the event of a loss of cabin pressure," says the stewardess with a straight face, "please affix your own oxygen mask first before helping the cat with his."

I cannot help myself. I begin laughing out loud. "It would almost be worth crashing to see you try to put an oxygen mask on a cat," I tell the cat lady. She laughs as if it's the funniest joke she's heard in

---

[1] I do not know to this day if this is an inside stewardess joke. It took them a while to bring our drinks, so I bet they locked themselves in the cockpit to laugh about it.

years. And for the rest of the flight we are friends. All I can smell is cat food, but I have learned once again that laughter is the shortest distance between two people. The cat even seems happier.

Any pastor or missionary will tell you that the number one problem they face has nothing to do with theological differences. It involves people problems. Here are three ideas for dealing with problem people in your life.

1. Learn from them. The driver who cuts us off in traffic provides an excellent opportunity for us to resolve never to cut someone else off. The cranky boss who loves to chew us out shows us how not to treat others if ever we are in charge. And the person who simply refuses to be agreeable or even to agree to disagree teaches us how to adapt and move on. So send them each a thank-you note for helping you become a stronger person. Okay, maybe not. But don't let such opportunities be wasted. Don't let them wear you down; let them build you up instead.

2. Pray for them. When Jesus said in Luke 6:27–31 to love your enemies, he also advised us to "pray for those who mistreat you." We have both discovered the incredible power of praying for those who have wronged us. We'd tell you more about it, but they may be reading this book and know where our cars are parked.

3. Show them grace. If we're honest, we'll admit that a little bit of jerk resides in us all. We all need piles of pardon and plenty of patience and a daily bath in grace. So why not extend to others the grace we would want extended to us? Some of the softest people we know have the gruffest exteriors. Beneath sandpaper personalities may be someone who needs to witness a little grace, acceptance, and forgiveness themselves so they can quit being so judgmental of others. So go ahead and, whenever possible, do your best to wage peace.

Am I not destroying my enemies when I make friends of them?
Abraham Lincoln

He was a great patriot, a humanitarian, a loyal friend;
provided, of course, he really is dead.
Voltaire

Unfaithful Friends

A true friend is one who overlooks
your failures and tolerates your successes.
Doug Larson

It is in the character of very few men
to honor without envy a friend who has prospered.
Aeschylus

Friends. When you find good ones, they're worth their weight in gold. As the old saying goes, "Friends know you're a good egg even though you're slightly cracked." Friends will stay by your side when everyone else runs away, or cheer for your successes and weep for your disappointments and hurts. Friends will watch your back when you don't even know there are incoming arrows. Friends know you better than you know yourself. Friends will laugh with you and let you grow. Friends will let you know when you're emotionally stuck over a hurtful situation or relationship. Friends won't let you fail or get off track. Friends will encourage you and let you vent. Friends will pray with you. Friends will join you in blowing your diet, then help you get back on it! Friends will let you doubt. Friends will feel your pain. Friends will remind you of your worth every time you forget it. And there are those really close friends who will tell us when there's mustard on our chin.

So how do you know the difference between a good friend and a bad friend?

Desirable Friend	Undesirable Friend
Invites you to dinner.	Invites you to dinner . . . at a different restaurant than where he's eating.
Buys some doughnuts and shares them with you.	Buys some doughnuts and shares them with you. He eats the doughnuts, you get the box.
Sends you a birthday card.	Sends you a belated birthday card that lists old songs you'll be able to identify with now . . .

B. J. Thomas—"Hair Plugs Keep Fallin' Off My Head"
Roberta Flack—"The First Time Ever I Slipped a Disc"
Johnny Nash—"I Can See Double Now"
Celine Dion—"My Heart Will Skip On"
Adriana Caselotti—"Someday My Gout Will Come"
The Bee Gees—"Saturday Night Nightsweats"
The Fortunes—"Here Comes That Rainy Day Stiffness Again"
Blue Swede—"Hooked On an IV"
Paul Simon—"Fifty Ways to Lose Your Dentures"
Leo Sayer—"You Make Me Feel Like Napping"

Apologizes for letting months go by without speaking to you. Time just got away from him.	*Apologizes for not speaking to you for months. He says, "I didn't want to interrupt you."*
Sees you're depressed and cheers you up.	*Sees you are about to jump off a cliff and runs after you, yelling, "Wait! Since you're obviously going to be busy for a while, mind if I borrow your car?"*
Hears someone gossiping about you and defends you.	*Not only lets you sizzle on the gossip rotisserie, but offers to turn you every so often so you'll broil more evenly.*
Gives you their shoulder to lean on.	*Gives you their shoulder to lean on . . . because it's easier to get you in a headlock that way.*

One of the side benefits of living long enough is that we will probably experience rejection by someone we thought to be a friend. When I (Phil) was a kid, even my imaginary friend dropped me! But it's no laughing matter. Rejection can take years to overcome. What we have both experienced is that forgiveness is a daily choice (and sometimes minute by minute). We have also learned that when thoughts of tarring and feathering come to mind, one thing will make all the difference. If we take those thoughts that are inward and outward and turn them upward, we will be changed for the better.

There is no revenge so complete as forgiveness.
Josh Billings

I am not of that feather, to shake off
my friend when he must need me.
William Shakespeare

Even Steven

**I don't want everyone to like me;
I should think less of myself if some people did.**
Henry James

If we're having a difficult time blessing our enemy, we're probably fighting the temptation to get even, too. Now, while we certainly don't promote this type of vengeful behavior (remember God has said that vengeance is his, and he's a lot better at it than we ever could be), there are times when we may find ourselves sitting and thinking about some creative ways to even the playing field with those who have hurt us.

(Note: If you are feeling too pious to admit that thoughts of vengeance have ever crept into your head, skip to the end of this piece, where we have written a disclaimer reminding readers that it was all in good fun. But if you're human and honest like the rest of us, read on.)

Socially Acceptable Ways[1] to Get Even With the Mean and Nasty People in Your Life

Get a universal remote and stand outside their window switching TV channels.

Follow a few paces behind them, spraying everything they touch with a can of Raid.

Place a classified ad in the paper for a gigantic garage sale, listing cheap TVs, antiques, vintage automobiles, and the address of your victim. "Sale begins at 6:00 A.M. Most items in house. Please ring doorbell."

Get their bald spot listed with Ripley's Believe It or Not as a newly discovered crop circle. Quote the admission fee and visiting hours.

Put their cell phone number on speed dial and call it numerous times when they're golfing.

Find out where they shop, then buy and wear exactly the same outfits.

Call restaurants and make reservations in their name.

Hug them and then tell them you're sure your poison ivy is all cleared up by now.

Switch their lawn furniture with their grouchy neighbors'. While the neighbor is still sleeping on it.

Stuff an orange into their exhaust pipe. Or better yet, the whole fruit tree.

Disclaimer: The above are intended for reading entertainment

[1]At least we think they are.

purposes only. Do not actually do any of them. And don't think about them for very long. At the first sign of a chuckle, go immediately back to thinking about "Whatever is true, whatever is noble, whatever is right, whatever is pure, whatever is lovely, whatever is admirable . . . think about such things" (Philippians 4:8).

Speak well of your enemies, sir, you made them.
Oren Arnold

An eye for an eye makes the whole world blind.
Gandhi

Out of the Dust

If the world seems cold to you, kindle fires to warm it.
Lucy Larcom

When a little boy's grandmother died, his mother told him that
Grandma had gone to be with Jesus. "But what about her
body?" asked the child. His mother thought for a second and
then told him, "It returned to dust." The little boy didn't seem
to let it bother him. But a few months later he came running
into the living room. "Mama," he hollered, "Grandma's back. I
just opened the back door and she blew in all over the kitchen
floor!"

Dust has been known to visit our kitchens, too. It doesn't
take up a lot of room, and it takes only a broom or dustcloth
to get rid of it, but for the most part, dust is an unwelcome
presence.

Have you ever thought, however, about what God did with a little
bit of dust?

First of all, he created man from it: "The Lord God formed the
man from the dust of the ground and breathed into his nostrils the

70

breath of life, and the man became a living being" (Genesis 2:7).

He healed the blind man with it: "He replied, 'The man they call Jesus made some mud and put it on my eyes. He told me to go to Siloam and wash. So I went and washed, and then I could see'" (John 9:11).

And Jesus preached a sermon in it, shutting up the mouths of some self-righteous folk of that day when he bent down and started to write on the ground with his finger. You'll remember this story from the chapter on Pharisees.

And here you thought dust wasn't of much use; that it's just something we walk on. But God saw value in that which we walk on. Even though it was mere dust, it was still something he could use. In fact, he saw enough value in it to fashion us from it, heal a man with it, and teach the people an important lesson about grace. It's funny, isn't it, that God found a use for something we consider pretty insignificant, something we're inclined to discount and discard. You know what? He sees value in people who have been discarded and walked on, too.

We say, "He failed so miserably."
God says, "And you've never failed me?"
We say, "But look at her past."
God says, "I'd rather look at her future."
We say, "But you don't know what they did to me."
And God gently whispers, "I forgave those who nailed me to a cross."

If God still chooses to love the unlovely, shouldn't we love them, too?

If God still chooses to raise up those whom society walks on, maybe we should see the same value in them.

Forbear to judge, for we are sinners all.
William Shakespeare

The only service a friend can really render is
to keep up your courage by holding up to you a mirror
in which you can see a noble image of yourself.
George Bernard Shaw

Clearing Out the Fridge

Nothing so needs reforming as other people's habits.
Mark Twain

Once while I (Martha) was putting fuel in my car at a local gas station, my son drove by and saw me there. He pulled in and we started talking. When my tank was full, I said good-bye to him and drove off. I didn't get very far before hearing a loud noise behind me. Looking in my side mirror, I noticed something long and skinny hanging out of the side of my car. I also saw the gas tanks that were now a good hundred feet away from the tank. Unless an anaconda had somehow slithered up to my car and was taking a drink out of my tank, there was only one explanation for what I was seeing—I had forgotten to take the gas hose out before driving off, and I was now dragging it along beside me.

It's not always a good idea to hang on to things, is it? Luckily, the gas station forgave my carelessness. But often the things we hang on to in life aren't quite as innocent. We know exactly what we're doing every single time we drive off with our pain when we could have easily left it behind. But they're *our* wounds. Of course we want to hang on to them. We've carried those hurts for so long, we might not know what to do with ourselves if they weren't a part of our lives.

The main reason most of us don't let go of our pain is because we fear that letting go of it will change the fact that it happened in the first place. If we forgive those who've hurt us, will that mean they didn't hurt us? Of course not.

Jesus forgave the people who crucified him on the cross, but it didn't change the fact that he was hanging there. Forgiveness isn't denial. It just means we're not going to be carrying the hurt around any longer. We're going to leave the hose back at the gas station and go home and clear out the fridge—and our emotional baggage, too.

> Write injuries in dust, benefits in marble.
> *Benjamin Franklin*

> The injury we do and the one we suffer
> are not weighed in the same scales.
> *Aesop*

Prayer for My Enemies

Lord, thank you for my enemies.

    They sharpen me.

        They make me uncomfortable.

            They teach me about myself.

                Lord, thank you for my enemies.

    They show me why I should never gossip or spread irretrievable rumors.

        They help me spend more time in prayer.

            Praying for them and the weakness they bring out
in me.

You said I'd be forgiven just like I forgive, so I'll choose forgiveness right now.

    And half an hour from now when I want to take it back.

        And tomorrow, too.

            With your help.

IT'S ALWAYS Darkest BEFORE THE Fridge Door Opens

Lord, thank you for my enemies.
    They help me appreciate my friends.

While we may not be able to control all that happens to us,
    we can control what happens inside us.
    Benjamin Franklin

Joy Comes in the Mourning

Joy is the serious business of heaven.
C. S. Lewis

We should give as we would receive, cheerfully, quickly,
and without hesitation; for there is no grace in
a benefit that sticks to the fingers.
Seneca

Between the two of us, we have written some one hundred books. Some of these have hit bestseller lists; others have hit bargain bins. Mostly you will find our books in the humor section of bookstores and libraries. Or at the bottom of a broken desk leg, keeping the desk in balance.

Wherever you happen to find our books, we hope they've brought a few smiles your way. But don't think we don't try to write serious things, too. It's just that our train of serious thought only has a caboose. We both love to laugh and would rather make whatever points we feel we'd like to make through the avenue of humor.

Often complete strangers will come up to us and tell us a joke or a funny happening in their lives. We love and expect this. If after several hours they're still not done and they want to go home with us to finish telling the story, well, that can get a bit uncomfortable. But still, like we said, we have come to expect this and other odd but fun behaviors from our readers.

I (Phil) was sitting in a restaurant once when an autograph seeker came over and said, "Excuse me, would you mind . . ." and I said, as politely as I could, "Can this wait until after dinner?" The stranger looked at me funny and said, "I just wanted to borrow your salt shaker." I gave him the salt and an autograph. He had never heard of me and didn't really want the autograph, but I didn't want to come across as proud and not give him one.

Perhaps the most surprising thing is how often someone will come to us and tell us the single most tragic event of their lives. Laughter and tears are closely linked, it would seem. We're not sure why so many people will share their needs with us. Perhaps they sense that humorists can laugh about almost anything, and they want us to help them find what they can laugh about in their lives, too. Sometimes, though, they will tell us a story that stops us in our tracks, and we can't stop thinking about it for days. One of those events took place a hundred miles from Phil's front door, and the results are still being tallied.

On a dark February night, fourteen-year-old Daniel Garrard took the family van out for a joyride, collided with a semitrailer, and was killed. Daniel's mother, Terra, and his three siblings were devastated. As a single mother, Terra worked hard in a grocery store to make ends meet, but without a car and without hope, despair closed in around her.

Two teens, Katelin Allert and Amy Fitzpatrick, were watching, though. And they wondered what they could do to help their co-worker. How about a fund-raiser? Maybe they could help her buy a van.

At first the dream seemed impossible. For one thing, the logistics would have challenged a *professional* fund-raiser. But the two teenagers began to plan. First, they convinced the manager of the grocery store where they worked to give them five hundred dollars. They used the money to put down a deposit on the best venue in town. Next, they began visiting business after business asking for an auction item or a donation. Something surprising began to happen.

"Before we went into each one, we prayed," recalls Katelin. "Only one business in the whole city turned us down."[1]

At her irresistible urging, Katelin's father, Gord, a guitar virtuoso, began inviting musician friends to come and play at the event. Gladly they hopped on planes. Country star Paul Brandt heard about it and donated an autographed guitar. And Gord asked me (Phil) to speak. I knew I couldn't say no, but what would I speak about? A comedian speaking at a fund-raiser for a young teen who had died such a tragic death?

When Katelin and her mom, Liz, shared the plans with Terra, she was overwhelmed. Liz and Katelin took her shopping for a new outfit to wear at the event. Daniel's mom also expressed interest in a Bible, so they gladly gave her one. As the community heard what was happening, tickets began selling fast. On a Sunday evening in June, three hundred people gathered to support this family in their grief. Standing before them, I talked of joy— how it had invaded our lives when we couldn't explain it. I told them of the peace I'd found in walking with Christ, how happiness depends on what happens but joy does not. We cried together and prayed together.

And as we prayed, the true Christlike actions of these two

---

[1]We're not mentioning the name, but it's right there beside the yogurt place on Third. Just kidding.

young girls began to bear fruit. The results were nothing short of miraculous.

We'll let the local newspaper tell you more.

Garrard Touched by Community Support

Hundreds attend benefit in memory of Daniel Garrard, that includes one big surprise

An Evening of Music, Humor and Hope turned into an evening of triumph on Sunday night as hundreds turned out in support of the Garrard family. And, in a move that was known about by only a select few, not only was money raised to support Terra Garrard, but a van from Cochrane Dodge turned out to be a part of the night. "They called me and my family on stage and said they had a little gift they wanted to give me," said a still emotional Garrard on Monday. "They handed me a little bag, and inside were the keys to a van." For Garrard the support was "overwhelming."[2]

What the paper didn't report is that during the next few weeks, Terra couldn't stop asking questions. But instead of "why?" she began asking "Who?" Who could be behind people loving her the way they had? Who could be there to comfort her in her lonely hours? Who could make all the pain she was feeling ever go away?

As Terra struggled with grief, she began to wonder if what she had seen in Katelin and Amy was worth having for herself. She began reading the Bible that Liz had given to her. On one of her most difficult days, she called the pastor to say, "I need to talk to you, now!" Arriving at the church, she asked Pastor Jason to introduce her to Jesus. Jason grinned. Nothing would please him more.

---

[2]*Cochrane Times*, May 16, 2005.

Ask Katelin and Amy what effect this has had on them, and they'll grin, too. For they have seen God at work. And whenever we see what God is doing, despite our doubts, despite our weaknesses, despite our pain, we can't help but be changed forever.

I (Martha) once received a letter from the aunt of a young *Brio* magazine reader who was putting together a book for her niece, Anne Farris, on what the meaning of *success* was. She was writing to different people, asking them to write a response before compiling all the letters into a booklet for Anne.

I answered the letter, saying that I thought the meaning of success was being in the center of God's will for your life. A short while later I received another letter. It was a thank-you note from Anne, saying what my letter had meant to her. As I started to put the note back into the envelope, I noticed something else in there. I pulled it out. It was Anne's obituary. Anne had died suddenly while running laps. She was only fifteen years of age. When I wrote to the address on the envelope, I said how sorry I was to hear about Anne's death. Anne's mother wrote me back and asked me if I had ever considered writing a book for teens on dealing with death.

I ran the idea past my publisher and we broadened it to include divorce, death of different family members, death of a pet, moving away, and other kinds of losses. It was called *Saying Goodbye When You Don't Want To,* and it is filled with letters from people, young and old, who have had grief in their lives and how they got through it. I think both Anne and Daniel would be pleased to know that through their tragic deaths, so many others have been and are being encouraged and reminded of God's unfailing love.

The greatest pleasure I know is to do a good action
by stealth, and to have it found out by accident.
Charles Lamb

To do the useful thing, to say a courageous thing, to contemplate
the beautiful thing: that is enough for one man's life.
T. S. Eliot

PART THREE

Chill First, Then Serve

(You Can't Be a Smart Cookie If You Have a Crummy Attitude)

> Brain cells come and brain cells go,
> but fat cells live forever.
> *Gord Robideau*

So much of life is about attitude. Do we wake up each morning saying, "This is the day that the Lord has made, let us rejoice and be glad in it"? Or do we wake up and say, "This is the alarm clock that Wal-Mart has made, let us send it sailing out the window and be glad it's gone"?

We can either go through our day looking for things to go wrong, or we can look for things to go right. The title of this section is "Chill First, Then Serve." It's about the importance of maintaining a good attitude. Sometimes before we can serve others, we first need to learn how to chill, go with the flow, adapt, and be the one who, win or lose, can always be counted on to have a smile on our face.

Last Nerves

*Most people are about as happy as
they make up their minds to be.*
Abraham Lincoln

How many times have you found yourself on your very last nerve? You're not really sure what your daily allotment of nerves is, but one by one they have been getting killed off, and now that you're down to your last one, you feel it's only fair to warn everyone within earshot, "I'm down to my last nerve!"

You wish you could have given them an earlier warning, sort of like what they do with tornadoes, and have a siren go off, but we humans tend to run out of nerves so quickly, it's hard to know when we're on the last one. With tornadoes, the weather service can tell where rotation is happening in the clouds, and they can warn people accordingly. Nerves are a little trickier. People get on our nerves in so many places and situations throughout our day—at the mall, in rush-hour traffic, at work, at home, even in church. And without a chart telling us exactly how many nerves we're using up with each encounter, how can we possibly keep a good tab on how many we have left? That's what the world needs. A nerve chart, like one of those gas gauges on a car that will show you exactly how many more miles you can go before you run out of gas. Think of the frustration we could save our-selves if a chart like this was in existence. Well, we're tired of waiting for someone to come out with such a chart, so we have developed our own. . . .

Nerve Depletion Chart

Action	Nerves Used
Telemarketer calling during dinner	4
Girl tallying your groceries, chewing a wad of gum, and talking on her cell phone	6
Inattentive waiter	3
Phone conversation with a whiner	5
Phone conversation with a braggart	8
Door-to-door salesman who won't take no for an answer	7
Appliance calls it quits	5
Stuck between two noisy parties on camping trip	9
Noisy parties are playing rap "music"	17
Children poking each other in backseat of car	9
Son throws daughter's iPod out car window	12
Daughter throws son out car window	30
Major car trouble (your car is at exit 136, the engine is at exit 135)	35
Man cuts in front of you on the freeway	12
Tie cut off in paper cutter	36

The above list isn't by any means complete, but we hope it gives you an idea of how quickly our nerves can get depleted throughout the day. It's no wonder most of us are already on our last one by noon. Thankfully, there are other events we encounter that scientists believe can actually replace those beaten-down nerves.

Nerve Replenishment Chart

Action	Nerves Replenished
Check in the mail	12
Someone saying thank-you	18
Encouraging word	22
Call from good friend	30
Unexpected raise or promotion	37
Someone really *listening* to you	24
A hearty laugh at a good clean joke	25
A repaired relationship	45
Hug from a loved one	50
Son buys daughter new iPod	78
Daughter visits son in hospital to apologize for car window incident	341

The apostle Paul reminds us in Philippians 4:4–6 to "Rejoice in the Lord always. I will say it again: Rejoice! Let your gentleness be evident to all. The Lord is near. Do not be anxious about anything, but in everything, by prayer and petition, with thanksgiving, present your requests to God." Did you notice that Paul said that we are to rejoice *always*? Is he kidding? Rejoice in the middle of what I'm going through? No way!

Yes way. How could he say that? Because he's been in those difficult places, too. In fact, Paul was writing these words from prison, where he had every reason to be on his last nerve. Yet he chose to focus on three irrefutable truths for the weary and worn down. Three truths that can bring joy, peace, even laughter to our lives, in the midst of our circumstances.

1. Rest in peace. Your Father is awake. Why should you be, too? He has promised that we will never have to walk through our disappointments, hurts, and frustrations alone. He will be there. So we can close our eyes at night and get the rest we need.

2. Worry is a waste of good time. You know what they say, worry is like a rocking chair. It gives you something to do, but it will never take you anywhere. And what's the cure for worry—prayer. God hears us when we bring our anxieties to him. So quit biting those fingernails. God didn't intend for fingernails to be food.

3. Be thankful. Joy grows best in the soil of thanksgiving. Even when you're down to your last nerve, even when life is unfair, even when no one understands where you're coming from, even when you're being lied about, God has a way of sending nerve replenishers into our lives. People who counter every attack, every discouraging word, every hurt, and every disappointment. We won't always recognize them (nerve replenishment often comes from people we don't even know or expect anything from), but these stealth encouragers are secretly and steadily rebuilding our stock of nerves so that we'll be able to face another day. God sends these nerve replenishers into our lives at just the right moment.

Another good way to replenish our own nerves is to go in search of those who could use some nerve replenishing from us. You can't help rebuild someone else's nerves and not have a positive effect on your own.

And then, with a restored nerve system, when our tie gets

caught in the paper cutter, we'll still be able to find something to be thankful for. At least it wasn't our tongue.

What do we live for,
if it is not to make life less difficult for each other?
George Eliot

Empty Shelves

It may be that your sole purpose in life
is simply to serve as a warning to others.
Steven Wright

Reality. It's a great place to visit, but do we really have to live there? I (Martha) once wrote a country lyric called, "The State of Denial." It's about moving back to the state of Denial because it's a much nicer place to live. We don't have to face the fact that our loved one lost their battle with cancer. We don't have to deal with our job loss, our relationship breakup, a son or daughter's poor choice, or any other factor of reality. The harder life gets, the higher the population grows in the state of Denial. It's like our mothers used to tell us, "Denial isn't just a river in Egypt." It's a place where all's right and well with the world.

The problem with living in such a state is the fact that not much happens there. We're frozen in time, and if you've ever experienced a Canadian winter, as Phil has,[1] you know that the

---

[1]Forty-four of them, in fact.

only thing that grows when it's frozen is water. There's an old saying that goes like this: "Calm seas never made a great sailor." How true it is. Growth almost always comes from the storms of life—from the pain we go through. If you're like us, we're not always looking for that kind of growth! We'd like calm seas and pristine sunsets and a daily buffet of good things. Prefer it, really. We'd like warmth in our hearts and full shelves in our refrigerators. But while these are nice, they are not always possible. We can console ourselves with the fact that difficulty helps us grow, that we're not here to wilt but to bloom. That we don't want to be twenty-six years old and still wearing toddler sizes, so the growth is helpful.

All isn't right and well with the world. We're going to get hurt, we're going to be disappointed, we're going to have problems come crashing into our lives without warning or welcome. And like it or not, we're going to grow and learn something from them all.

Life is a succession of lessons. . . .
Ralph Waldo Emerson

Welcome to Whine Country

It is no use to grumble and complain;
it's just as cheap and easy to rejoice.
James Whitcomb Riley

I (Phil) am a chronic complainer. I grumble. I gripe. I have grievances. I open the fridge and find things there like grouse, carp, and sour grapes. Sometimes my whining gets on my wife's nerves. She says, "You should quit whining, Phil." But I tell her, "I'm not whining. And why do you always have to pick on me? And why aren't there any apples left in the fridge? And what happened to my favorite cheese? And why isn't there any iced tea made? And why are you nagging me about my whining?" I hate to admit it, but I have won the Wimbledon of whining and the Grand Slam of bellyaching all in the same week. These are the things I have found myself complaining about lately:

The water from our tap. It leaves smudges on our cups.

Mosquitoes. Big enough to ride.[1]

---
[1]And show up on radar.

Why I have to follow my teenagers around the house shutting
lights off. It's a full-time job.

Long waits in doctors' offices with mediocre reading material.[2]

The weather, which includes snow in late April.

Why the garbage truck never comes on time.

The twenty-nine mateless socks in my sock drawer. Where are their
poor partners? Is it true missing socks form the ring on Saturn?
And why didn't they tell me they were having problems staying
together? I could have gotten them into counseling.

Why all four wheels on my shopping cart go in opposite directions.
Don't they know that a shopping cart divided against itself cannot
roll?

The warning at the start of the movie that says, "This movie has
been formatted to fit your screen." Of course it's reformatted. My
screen is fourteen inches wide.

How far I have to drive to church and why all the slow drivers
switch lanes at precisely the same moment I do. And why doesn't
someone come out with a separate "cell phone lane" and let the
rest of us drivers get on our way?

Why we have a channel devoted completely to the weather and
still they can't get it right. I'm in rainstorms with no umbrella,
snowstorms while dressed in shorts, and heat waves so intense I
have no choice but to remove my parka. Can't someone just tell me

---

[2]Although it sure beats a mediocre doctor with great reading material.

for sure what the weather is going to do so that I can dress appro-
priately and not waste ten bucks driving my car into an automatic
car wash on a sunny day only to drive out at the other end per-
fectly cleaned and waxed just as the monsoon hits?

I think my whining might get on God's nerves once in a
while, too. Maybe that's partly the reason he allowed my wife
and I and two of our three children to take a trip to a Third-
World country (with the organization Compassion) right in the
middle of the writing of this book. He knew how petty and hol-
low some of my complaints were going to sound in the face of
real poverty and need.

"Who moved my stapler?!" seems to shrink in importance
when compared to "Daddy, why don't we have anything to eat
again tonight?"

Some children don't stand at the fridge wondering what's for
supper because there is no fridge. There is no supper.

On our trip, I held children who were orphaned when their
fathers were electrocuted trying to tap into power lines so the
family could have one bare light bulb in their house.

We stood in a village that a hurricane had completely leveled,
except for a church and the Compassion building. They told me
the miraculous story with faces beaming. Yes, they'd lost everything. Yes, their homes had blown away. But the church was still
standing.

And there I stood in mid-grumble. The guy who gripes about
the weather and lights left on and waiting on doctors. These
people have never seen a doctor. I'm the guy with trivial complaints like the fact that my hair has gone underground and
begun coming out my ears. What on earth do I have to complain
about? My grumbling had been the death of my thanksgiving.

On the day we visited our sponsored child Carlos, the temperature was almost unbearable and we ran out of bottled water.

Never in my short life had I experienced such raging thirst. Suddenly Carlos' stepmother pulled from a small icebox the greatest gift imaginable: an ice-cold bottle of Coca-Cola. I ran my fingers over that bottle and giggled like a fourth grader who had just heard the funniest joke imaginable. I held that bottle up to the light, then sipped it slowly, relishing every single drop as they crawled one by one down my eager throat. This drink was nectar straight from heaven. This drink was a companion and a friend and a teacher. It taught me to give thanks for each and every blessing while we hold it in our hand.

So on the long flight home, while the "formatted to fit your screen" movie was playing, I wrote a list of things I'm thankful for after having been in the Third World:

Water that comes out of a tap. And it's the color water should be.

A bed without large spiders in it. Especially when they hog all the blankets.

Lights in the house. Even if they're on too much.

"Dot havig to plug by dose." The assault on my nasal passages as we traveled through some of these communities was unbearable.

Waiting for the doctor and knowing he's in. We bellyache because we have to wait an hour in a doctor's comfortable waiting room complete with leather sofas, aquarium, and hope. Most of the people I met don't have access to simple medical cures we take for granted every day.

The weather, even that late April snowstorm.

Single socks. I'll find mates for them. Even if I have to fly to Saturn someday.

Garbage dumps outside our cities. They may not always be on time picking up the trash, but at least we don't have to share sidewalk space with it indefinitely.

Shopping carts and grocery stores crammed with food. In my entire life, I don't think I've ever had to literally go to bed hungry. Dieting doesn't count.[3] I will purge "I'm starving" from my vocabulary.

Driving to church. If we had to walk, I wonder how many of us would show up.

Family. Life is so fragile in these countries. So many have lost their loved ones to disease and uprisings. It certainly makes you appreciate the ones you love.

A place to sleep tonight.

And a toothbrush and comb, even if I need only one of them.

I wish I could say that my recent trip to that Third World country cured all of my whining. But sadly, I still find myself slipping back into my old ways. Maybe the car in front of me isn't moving fast enough, or the lady at the bank made a mistake on my account again, or I can't bring myself to drink the recommended amount of eight glasses of water a day because it's too much of a bother to get up and walk over to the sink and turn on the tap. Things still happen throughout my day that push my Whine button. But more and more I'm trying to stop myself in

---

[3]Being sent to bed without dessert doesn't count, either. Nor does being "still hungry" after a full seven-course meal.

mid-whine and remember the lessons learned on that trip. How truly blessed I am.

Satan is a chronic grumbler.
The Christian ought to be a living doxology.
Martin Luther

Ten Things We'd Like to Hear Someone Say

1. You know, I have way too many close friends. I don't know what to do with them all.

2. I guess we have enough money now. It's time to give some away.

3. I've been spending way too much time with my children. I think they need a break.

4. I'm all caught up at work. I don't know what to do now.

5. I'm getting bald, but that's okay. I'll worry about what's going on *inside* my head.

6. I'm having to get my knees replaced. An old prayer injury.

7. I've decided to find out who's gonna cry at my funeral and

hang out with them instead of those who probably won't even show up to it anyway.

8. I'm so excited! I found another laugh line on my face this morning!

9. Television? Are you kidding? With so many good books to read?

10. I know the speed limit is seventy, but I'm going to drive in the slow lane and just enjoy the scenery. At least until that cop behind me passes.

Slice of Life

Those who do not feel pain seldom think that it is felt.
Samuel Johnson

Do you remember sitting at the dinner table comparing slices of pie? Remember how your brother (or sister or cousin or the one doing the slicing) always seemed to get a more generous wedge of lemon meringue? "Hey, that's not fair!" we yelled.[1] Do you remember sitting in school comparing smarts during final exams, asking why God didn't give you more brains? Did you ever wonder why a friend always seemed to get the perfect job, the newer car, or the bigger bank account? "Life isn't fair," your mother told you. Which didn't really seem like a fair answer. But then there comes a time in life when you are shocked, and more than a little disappointed, to discover that she was right.

While golfing with my friend James, I (Phil) was robbed. Not by a masked man on a golf cart, but by a more unusual suspect.

---

[1] Even now that we're all on diets, we still might do it, only we're not as indignant over who gets the biggest carrot.

On the seventh hole on our little town's course,[2] James and I were stunned to hit the green with our third shots (for those of you who think golf is a four-letter word, we made uncharacteristically good shots). As we walked toward the hole with birdies[3] on our minds, something even more stunning happened. A large raven descended from the sky and landed on the green. Then, as you've probably guessed, the miserable bird took flight with James' golf ball in its beak. It flapped out of sight, dropped the ball somewhere, then returned for mine. I still don't know the rules for such a predicament. But I realized once again that life is not fair. Neither is the game of golf.

You know what we mean. See how many of the following scenarios you can identify with:

Your new car gets hit at the mall. There's a note on your windshield that says, People think I'm leaving you my phone number. I'm not. Ha ha ha, sucker!

You fail the eye chart test you studied for all month. The guy before you who just winged it passed with a perfect 20-20 score. Why didn't God give you perfect vision, too?

You finish a glorious morning of work, writing brilliantly about solutions to the world's problems. This is the best and most creative work you've done in years. Your boss will be proud. Then before you can print it out, your computer crashes.

You are the most faithful parent on your daughter's basketball team. You attend every one of the games and even the practices. But the entire season she only sits on the bench while the less faithful are put in the games simply because they're better players. Or they're the coach's kids.

---

[2]It's a 527-yard par five. Golfers like to know these things.
[3]This is another golfing term, which means that your hopes are about to be dashed.

You've worked hard year after year in the same job, only to watch a lazy co-worker get promoted.

A loved one is diagnosed with a serious illness in the same year that your car gets repossessed and the bank forecloses on your house. Then you get a call from your boss that the company is downsizing and they're laying you off.

You don't get invited to the party of the year, even though everyone else you know does.

Someone lies about you.

Hurtful, unfair situations. In fact, that's what makes them so painful. The fact is that you don't deserve any of it.

But we can't talk about life's fairness without looking at the flip side of the coin. Sometimes good things do happen to good people. Even on the golf course.

Gene Perret, a fellow writer and good friend, once told Martha, "It's like my golf: sometimes I'll hit a poor shot that slams into a house along the course, bounces off the roof and back onto the course, hits a metal sprinkler head and pops way up in the air, lands in a tree and skids down one of the branches, landing on the paved cart path, rolls down the hills, falls off the cart path, and trickles onto the green about six feet from the hole. I accept that. But when I miss the putt by two inches, I complain that life isn't fair."

Whether or not we play golf, we can all identify, can't we? When life's unfair and it hurts us, we hate it. When life's unfair and it's to our advantage, we're loving it. So the next time we begin to complain, perhaps it will help to remember a few of the undeserved blessings that have come our way, too.

The guy writing a note for your windshield not only leaves you his phone number but says he noticed the For Sale sign on your car and will give you five hundred dollars above the price you had in mind.

You win a contest you didn't even enter. A friend filled out the entry card for you.

Your son is daydreaming in left field, staring at his glove, when a deep fly ball miraculously lands in it, ending the game and giving your son's team the win.

Your old car makes it another fifty thousand miles.

Someone gives you their perfectly good refrigerator simply because they're buying a new one.

Your car comes to a screeching stop four inches from the car in front of you, the one you had been following too closely for the last twenty miles.

The IRS made a mistake. They actually owe you money.

No one invited you to the party because they are all coming to your house for a surprise party in your honor! And they are bringing the pizza.

One of the most glorious truths in all of Scripture is this: We don't get what we deserve. How thankful we should be that God is not fair. If he were, we'd all be in a heap of trouble. Even the self-righteous who think their failures aren't as bad as anyone else's. Especially the self-righteous. The Bible teaches that the wages of sin is death. If eternal life were "fair," if it were a reward based on our good qualities and the abundance of our good works, no one would ever see heaven.

So next time you're tempted to observe that life is not fair, remember to thank God that we don't get what we deserve. We get something far better.

God saved you by his special favor when you believed.
And you can't take credit for this; it is a gift from God.
Salvation is not a reward for the good things we have done,
so none of us can boast about it.

Ephesians 2:8–9 NLT

I prayed this morning, but I didn't pray to win.
I just thanked God to be alive. You know, the everyday stuff.
I've never prayed to win a tournament. I don't think that
would be fair. Why should he show partiality toward me?

Rev. Walter Jessup,
after winning his second straight clergyman's golf tournament

The Best News Yet

Reflect upon your present blessings,
of which every man has plenty; not on your
past misfortunes of which all men have some.

Charles Dickens

I (Phil) visited a barbershop recently. My daughter asked me why. "There's nothing happening up there, Dad" is how she put it. "There's a recession going on right on top of your head." Teenagers. They get a little older and they won't know so much. I smiled at her. And cut her out of the will.

When I arrived at the barbershop, the hairdresser walked around my head once or twice, then squinted uncomfortably at me. I watched the ordeal in the mirror.

She said, "Um . . . do you have a part?"

I said, "Yes, it starts at my left ear and goes to my right."

She was still squinting. She said, "Would you like me to dye it?"

I said, "No, you look fine to me, you don't need to lose a pound."

The squint vanished and she smiled, then chuckled softly.

"Just a little off the top," I coached her.

It was her turn. "That's all you have," she said.

Did you ever have a haircut you wished you could get a refund on? In Oregon a mother recently threatened to sue the West Linn-Wilsonville school district because her eight-year-old boy returned home one day with "next to nothing" on his head. An employee had cut the boy's hair without permission. The mother said she tried to keep her son's hair looking neat but "there was one stinking day, and I'm not lying, that I didn't brush his hair." The district's insurance company paid a ten thousand dollar settlement.

I remember some really bad haircuts when I was a boy. My father used to start on one side of my head, then walk around to the other side and, relying on memory, try to even it up. I ended up wearing a hat for two weeks. Then my father would cut it again.

They say that the difference between a good haircut and a bad one is about two weeks. But surgery is another matter. Most major surgeries don't allow you to go back and fix something. And you can't just put on a hat and make the pain go away. My older brother Dan went through the horrible ordeal of a detached retina recently.[1] Just before the operation, a nurse leaned over and said, "It's your left eye, right?" Dan was stunned. It was his right eye. He knew this absolutely for sure. The nurse frowned and squinted at a computer printout. "It says here it's your left eye."

"No, it's not," said Dan, "I can see fine with my left eye; please don't operate on it."

Of course, we're able to laugh a little later about such things. But what about when the news is the worst possible? When a trip

---

[1]Complicated by the fact that the NBA playoffs were on.

to the doctor changes everything we've taken for granted? While speaking at a banquet, I sat next to Ed, an oil executive, who told me his amazing story. One year earlier he sat in his doctor's office listening but unable to process the doctor's horrible words. At the age of forty-nine, he had colon cancer. The shock had only begun to set in as the doctor explained it to Ed's wife. "The cancer is very advanced. I've seen other cases like this, and it's highly unlikely that your husband's body can fight it more than six months. We'll do all we can to help him, but he had better get his affairs in order. I'm so sorry."

After a sleepless night, Ed called his office. For the first time in seventeen years he would not be at work. His work meant everything to him; what would he do without it? He wondered how he would tell his three grown children. Though they lived nearby, they were almost strangers now. And what about the grandchildren? Would they even care? Though he had his secretary mail them birthday and Christmas gifts of her choosing, he seldom saw them, and he'd never been able to get their names straight. *Should I call a minister?* he wondered. But church hadn't been a part of his life since his wedding day. He hadn't the time for it. Besides, who would he call? What would he say?

Thankfully Ed was wrong about all his apprehensions. His children were devastated by the news of his illness. For the first time ever they saw their father reduced to tears. And they heard the words he'd never told them: "I love you." That night, an old friend from college called. He'd heard the news. He was a minister. Could they go out for breakfast? How did eight o'clock sound?

The next day after breakfast, Ed booked twelve tickets to Mexico, enough to take his children, their spouses, and all the grandchildren for two weeks. It was a Christmas like no other.

Though the doctor had done a painful colonoscopy, leaving Ed barely able to sit on the airplane, he had the time of his life.

Surrounded by family, he began to wonder where he'd been all these years. He watched them frolic in the surf. He even went hang gliding.

"It was the best two weeks of my life," he told me. "I didn't start living until I knew I was dying."

Back home he went to see his doctor. He had never been ushered into a doctor's office so quickly. Seated behind a desk, the doctor's face was the color of a snowball. "Ed, I don't know how to tell you this, but we've made a terrible mistake. We . . . uh . . . got the files mixed up. You're healthy as a horse."

Ed couldn't bear to hope that the doctor's words were true. He sat still, unable to utter a word.

Finally he said, "You're probably wondering about a lawsuit, aren't you?"

"Frankly," said the doctor, "we are."

Ed smiled.

"How could I sue?" he asked. "You see, Doctor, I was a workaholic. The only thing I valued was money. It was all I could see. Then came your diagnosis. It changed everything. I've made things right with my kids. I know my grandchildren's names now, and they know mine. I've made things right with God, too. I'm going to church again. I've never been more alive in my life. I can't thank you enough. The worst news I ever received was also the best."

Getting up from his chair, he embraced the most surprised and grateful doctor in the history of medicine. Health is a gift, to be sure, but forgiveness, and a new grasp on what's truly important in life, is even better.

> Adversity can make us better. We must be challenged to
> improve, and adversity is the challenger.
> *John Wooden*

I thank God for my handicaps for, through them, I have found myself, my work, and my God.

Helen Keller

Ten Lessons Learned in the Kitchen

1. When showing your house to a potential buyer, avoid cooking sauerkraut, fish, eggs, or brussels sprouts.
2. If left to themselves, cats will not make a kitchen any cleaner.
3. If left to themselves, children will not, either.
4. When it comes to hot dogs, the less known about the preparation, the better.
5. Leftovers will sometimes be leftover. Don't let that stop you from disguising them in something else.
6. Any casserole with the word *surprise* in the title (e.g., Tuna Surprise, Seafood Surprise, Church Potluck Surprise, or Surprise, Surprise) should be approached with caution.[1]
7. When adding liver pâté to any dish, less is always better.
8. Limburger cheese will never hear the words, "Hmmm . . .

---

[1]If you're at a potluck and you'd really like to try it, though, simply watch carefully who brought it and see if their children partake.

what smells so good in the kitchen?''
9. Your shirt is not a potholder. (A lesson learned the hard way by Martha's sister.)
10. And finally, always remember to make meals small enough to finish, big enough to share.

I find the great thing in this world is not so much where we stand, as in what direction we are moving. To reach the port . . . we must sail sometimes with the wind and sometimes against it— but we must sail, and not drift, nor lie at anchor.

Oliver Wendell Holmes

Balance Keeps the Fridge Shelves From Collapsing

Don't dig your grave with your own knife and fork.
English Proverb

A few years ago, *Men's Fitness* magazine accused the city of Houston of having a weight problem, naming it "America's Fattest City." A local bike club decided they weren't going to take this sitting down eating Twinkies, so they came up with the idea of holding a forty-mile bike rally through the city's downtown streets. Trouble was, registrations were slow in coming. So organizers settled on a solution: They offered participants free beer and tacos at the end of the race. We kid you not.

Now, those of you who have ever seen a picture of us might be thinking to yourselves: Yes, America has an obesity problem and it's widening, but what do you know about it? Your pictures look like you live on celery and rice cakes, and a few locusts.[1]

---

[1]The locusts are true, but only on Sundays.

First of all, for the record, we're not really all that thin. At least, not as thin as we used to be.[2] Secondly, if you consider us on the thin side, it's not because we're dieting. Frankly, we're suspicious of any word that begins with *die*. We are also suspicious of anyone who has something against carbohydrates. Some of our best friends are carbohydrates. The main problem we've found with dieting is that people on a diet often lose their sense of humor. And you know how we feel about a sense of humor. There is no swimsuit in the world that is worth losing laughter just to wear it on the beach for a few hours.[3]

With this in mind, we have decided to offer you some tips from the Phil and Martha School of Eating.

1. The vitality of vegetables. We both love pumpkin pie, carrot cake, zucchini bread, and popped corn. Vanilla is technically a vegetable and should be watered down with ice cream. Chocolate comes from trees, which, if you know much about agriculture, makes it a fruit. Fruit is good for you. Chocolate-dipped strawberries are a must for any diet. M&Ms contain vitamins A, C, and E. You can check the package. Those of you who prefer real vegetables should realize that they aren't always healthy. Have you ever choked on a piece of broccoli? Do you realize you could have died that moment if someone hadn't brought you that brownie to push it on down with? We say let the veggies tell their tales, but if they must be on our plates, disguise them as something else.

2. Selective studies. Be careful which studies you depend on for information. There is much contradictory information available today, and it's difficult to know who's telling us the truth. Which news report would you believe? The one informing us that dark chocolate contains antioxidants that can decrease blood pressure, improve circulation, stimulate our kidneys, lower our

---

[2]It's amazing what they can do with digital photography.
[3]Our swimsuits often cause laughter.

death risk from heart disease, and cause warm fuzzy feelings? Or the one that said chocolate causes depression in mice? The first one, of course. If the mice are depressed, they're probably watching too much TV. And they need to balance their dark-chocolate diet out with a little nougat.

We should also note that the study claiming that rhubarb sandwiches are the leading source of calcium is clearly false. Rhubarb is poison, except in a pie. Everyone knows that.[4] The one about coffee causing irritability is also sheer baloney and completely fabricated! We'd really like to know who thought it up!

When's the last time you saw a grouch at a Starbucks? If coffee can make the people there smile while they're paying those prices, it can't possibly cause irritability! We have also been so horrified by what we read about the effects of eating junk food that we almost gave up reading altogether.

3. The benefits of balance. Balance is what is needed when it comes to eating, and our idea of a balanced diet is a plate in each hand at the all-you-can-eat buffet.

Few areas of our lives can be more out of balance than the way we eat. Check any bestseller list and you'll find cookbooks there. Check that same list and you'll find dieting books. Imagine the irony. People buying books that instruct them how not to eat what they've just learned to cook.

When Jesus taught us to pray, he asked his Father for "our daily bread" (Luke 11:3). He did not say, "Give us this day our daily six meals complete with four courses and eight dessert choices."

When we were kids, our mothers would chide us for not cleaning our plates. "There are children in Africa that would give anything to be able to eat that food," they'd say, poking us with a fork, and we in our immaturity would think, *So mail it to them.*

---

[4]Rhubarb farmers of the world: Don't mail that letter, we were just kidding.

But once you've seen those African children, you'll find it hard to eat even a broken cookie without thanking God for the privilege.

Remember Jimmy Stewart's prayer in the movie *Shenandoah*? "Lord, we cleared this land, we plowed it, sowed it, and harvested it. We cooked the harvest. We worked dog hard for every crumb and morsel, but we thank you just the same anyway, Lord, for this food we're about to eat. Amen." We love Jimmy and we smile at such a prayer, but we think his character could have been a little more grateful.

Psalm 104:21 says, "The lions roar for their prey and seek their food from God." We would do well to remember that the earth's bounty and the grocery store's abundance are impossible without the Creator's gift of life. We are all dependent on God's grace and provision. One of his greatest biblical acts of grace is the feeding of the Israelites during their long trek from Egyptian slavery to the Promised Land. Manna appeared daily and could not be stored, reminding God's children of their daily dependence on him. We are dependent on God for our daily needs. And we should be thankful every time he meets them.

**If taking vitamins doesn't keep you healthy enough,
try more laughter.**
Nicolas-Sebastien Chamfort

In-Flight Misery

If I had to choose, I would rather have birds than airplanes.
Charles Lindbergh

I have found out there ain't no surer way to find out whether you
like people or hate them than to travel with them.
Mark Twain

If you've flown anywhere lately, you know what a challenge air
travel has become. If you're running late getting to the airport,
double that frustration. In most major cities, they advise you to
get to the airport at least two hours in advance of your flight
departure. We believe Los Angeles recommends two weeks. If
your business requires you to do a lot of traveling, as does ours (it
keeps us ahead of audiences wanting their money back), you
know all too well that in many cases, once you board the plane,
your troubles have just begun. But since this is a book about re-
capturing joy, we won't spend a lot of time on the negatives of
air travel. Comedian after comedian has already amply tackled
this topic.

Instead, what we want to do is provide you with a list of Ten New Ways to Look at Air Travel. Drawing from the truth that life is 3 percent what happens to you and 97 precent what you do with it, we are convinced that your air travel experiences will change if you can change how you look at them. You've got to open your mind and realize that maybe the airlines aren't out to make your life miserable just for the fun of it. That's part of it, certainly, but there may be plenty of other underlying reasons why they do what they do. Our inconvenience is a small price to pay for the rewards we will reap from looking at our next flight in the following new ways.

Ten New Ways to Look at Air Travel
1. Moving sidewalks.

Have you ever been walking on an airport moving sidewalk and found yourself wondering if you were moving all that much faster than the guy with the broken leg, pulling his Samsonite behind him, while balancing a latte with his teeth? Then, when he actually pulled ahead of you, did you start asking yourself why you even got on the moving sidewalk in the first place, but now you're trapped and can't do a thing about it?

The problem isn't the sidewalk, it's your focus. Instead of getting upset at the airlines for tricking you into stepping onto the moving sidewalk that doesn't seem to move you any faster than the slowest passenger strolling along beside you, look at it from the airline's point of view. Those moving sidewalks aren't there to get you to your gate faster than those who don't use it. They're simply to provide entertainment for the passengers who are stuck sitting at the gates waiting for their boarding calls. What else have they got to look at? Some rerun of a news item two weeks old? The man sitting across from them eating a boiled egg? The kids fighting with each other in the seats next to them? Let's face it, the entertainment at airports is very limited. So instead of complaining, start entertaining. Place your luggage down on the conveyor belt so that your hands will be free to wave at others as you pass by. Think of yourself as being on a parade float. Wave, sing, dance, do whatever you feel is appropriate. You might even want to juggle a few of those three-dollar airport candy bars in the air. In other words, enjoy the moment. And the opportunity to be discovered. *American Idol* and *Nashville Star* may reach millions, but who knows who might see you at an international airport. Music producers, movie directors, and even scouts for the Ringling Bros. circus all have to travel. They're walking airport terminals every day. So do your thing and who knows, you just might have a new career awaiting you. And one day you'll be able to say, "It all started in front of gate C-19!"

2. **Airplane seats that don't really recline but have a button making you think they do.**

The real reason for the uncomfortable seating on airplanes is obvious; you just have to look for it. Some think it's to sell all those neck rests and aspirin in the airport gift shop. Or to give chiropractors the much-needed business. But the real reason is to help you with your posture. So the next time the stewardess is playing that fun little game at landing, selecting people at random to tell them to bring their seat to the full upright position, play along and hit the button, even though you know it doesn't work. Your seat won't move, of course, but remember what the airlines know: Good posture is important. Uncomfortable, but important. Your back will thank you.

3. **Airline blankets.**

Yes, they are rough and can cut you to shreds in minutes if you move around too much beneath them. But these airline blankets are scratchy for a perfectly legitimate reason. While you may simply be cold and not have any rashes whatsoever, for those travelers who do, those blankets are actually a service that the airlines provide. Nothing scratches an itch like an airline blanket.

4. Individual air-conditioning controls.

We think it's cute how the airlines have led us to believe that we are actually controlling the cool-air flow to our individual seats. But if you've ever flown in the winter, you know that the cold air doesn't stop blowing on you no matter how tightly you close your vent. Icicles will form on your beverage cup, and you'll be begging the stewardess for a blanket, rash or not. But the airlines even have a good reason for this. The reason they make us think we can control the air flow above us is part of their fitness plan. They are helping all of us flabby-armed passengers work out those underarm muscles. On a three-hour flight, the typical passenger will do at least thirty of these arm lifts.

5. Airplane rest rooms.

If you're like the rest of us, you've probably spent a fair amount of time wondering why the rest rooms on an airplane are so small. Have the powers that be not looked at the size of the average passenger? We are not that little, and we are certainly not getting any smaller. If we were, airplanes would be able to fly at a much higher altitude. Some of us are taller than the tallest airplane rest room, wider than the width, and we haven't even begun to talk about claustrophobia. But believe it or not, they have a perfectly legitimate reason for small rest rooms, and it's an ecological one, too. It saves on paper towels. Plain and simple. The airlines know there's not enough room in there for you *and* a paper towel at the same time, so most passengers will simply opt for shaking out their hands a few times and air drying them with those overhead air-conditioning controls. This way, the airlines are saving money *and* trees. When you think about it in this manner, you will no longer be frustrated with the airlines but applaud their responsibility. This, of course, also compensates for all the money and water they waste at airport rest rooms from those toilets that automatically flush loudly (scaring you off your-seat) at least three times per visitor.

6. Lost luggage.

If you've ever had your luggage lost by an airline, you know what an inconvenience that can be. But it's not always negligence on their part. Sometimes it's a result of the fashion-savvy people who are present during your security check.

"He's not going to wear *that* suit to his business meeting, is he?"

"That dress went out of style years ago. What is she thinking? We can't let her wear that. Tag this suitcase and lose it immediately! It's our duty to save her from herself!"

They make us wait twenty-four hours or so, then give us a voucher to go out and buy some new clothes, hoping we'll visit different shops than we did during our last fashion excursion. If we do, we end up making quite the fashion statement, the fashion police will feel like heroes, and some underdeveloped country somewhere is getting regular donations of all these confiscated clothes. That's right, there's probably a village in some remote area of the world where everyone's walking around dressed like those kids in *That 70's Show*. But we're looking good![1]

7. Connecting gates as far apart as possible.

Again, this isn't simply to make our lives miserable. It's an exercise and physical fitness issue. You don't know this, but every time you're rushing to a connecting gate, you're being timed. Olympic scouts are posted at all major airports looking for possible contenders.

8. Airplane pillows the size of a Tic Tac.

Sure, we'd all like larger pillows whenever we're flying the red-

---

[1]Earlier we mentioned the theory that the ring on Saturn is made up entirely of single socks that have no mates. Now we're wondering if it consists of lost luggage, too.

eye, but think about it. Do you really want the guy next to you sleeping on a giant pillow that keeps knocking you in the face every time he tosses and turns? Of course not. Besides, if air travel was too conducive to sleep, think of all the drooling and snoring that would be going on. You'd never be able to hear the movie, much less the pilot telling you that engine three just died. The airlines are really doing us a favor by making the conditions so uncomfortable that we stay alert.

9. Security.

In this day and age, it goes without saying that we have to have tight security at our airports. But even this inconvenience can be looked upon with new eyes. Think of all the diseases and possible tumors they're finding early by the increased frisking and stronger X-ray machines. Or maybe they're causing them, we can't tell.

10. Airport parking.

It's a given that you can't park anywhere near the airport. So don't even bother complaining about it. Instead, think about all the exercising you're getting by dragging your suitcases, your child's car seat, and your jacket those three miles back to the airport. No gym on earth will give you that kind of a workout. And if it's in the middle of a hot Florida summer, you'll lose more water weight than from the best sauna around, and it won't cost you a single dime!

> There may be 50 ways to leave your lover,
> but there are only 4 ways out of this airplane.
> *Westjet flight attendant during safety announcement*

Driving Us Crazy

Bumper sticker: Stupidity is not a crime so you're free to go

We both love to drive. However, we sometimes encounter drivers that make us wonder if they received their license from their state as an April Fool's joke. We used to allow such people to stress us out whenever we encountered them on the road. But now we realize that it might not be their fault. Perhaps they did take and pass a driver's test, but theirs may have been just a little different than the one the rest of us take. That's why these drivers seem to be following different rules. They're not idiots. They were just handed a different test than we were. Theirs looked something like this:

1. Acceptable activities while driving include:

    a. *Conference calls*
    b. *Clipping toenails and applying nail polish*
    c. *Reading mail*
    d. *All of the above, simultaneously*

2. What are the left- and right-turn signals for?

   a. To keep time with the music on your radio
   b. To help you engage in the only exercise you'll get all day
   c. Suggested general direction of travel
   d. All of the above

3. How long should you remain in an intersection before executing a left-hand turn?

   a. No less than two light changes
   b. Until the honking grows unbearable
   c. Until your nap is over
   d. Until the Second Coming

4. If you hear a siren and see red or blue lights flashing behind you, this means you should immediately:

   a. Speed up and try to outrun them
   b. Stop suddenly and without warning, causing an accident; why waste a perfectly good ambulance?
   c. Smile. You're obviously in a movie!
   d. Start playing disco music

5. A curb painted red means:

   a. Your personal reserved parking space
   b. Someone tried to paint the town red but ran out of paint
   c. The town is getting ready for their annual running of the bulls
   d. The party is here

6. The mirrors in your car were installed to help you:

   a. Locate your children in the backseat so you can maintain eye contact when you yell at them
   b. Blind the person tailgating you with his brights on
   c. Apply mascara while you talk on the cell phone
   d. Make silly faces at the driver behind you

7. On the freeway, the left lane is for:

    a. *Underage drivers only*

    b. *Tractors*

    c. *Tourists*

    d. *Underage tourists driving tractors*

8. When choosing a parking spot on Christmas Eve, it is important to:

    a. *Give up any thought of finding one*

    b. *Borrow a handicapped sticker from a friend*

    c. *Get there in early November*

    d. *Remember what state you park in so you'll be able to find your car after shopping*

9. If you're running late getting to the airport, it is permissible to:

    a. *Become airborne*

    b. *Yell things at complete strangers*

    c. *Cut corners at Mach 1*

    d. *All of the above*

10. A raccoon crosses the road directly in front of you. You should:

    a. *Hit the ditch, but miss him*

    b. *Hit the brakes and cause a twelve-car pileup, but miss him*

    c. *Actually aim for the raccoon, chasing it off the road and up a tree*

    d. *Stop and ask it for directions*

11. A carload of teenagers driving next to you is making fun of the way you drive. You should:

    a. *Speed up to thirty-five miles per hour*

    b. *Speed up, cut them off, and lob a bran muffin at them*

c. *Challenge them to a race. Your moped can beat anything on the road!*

d. *All of the above*

12. Posted speed limits are:

a. *To let trucks know how fast the cars are traveling so they can gauge their speed accordingly in order to ride their tails*

b. *To be doubled and a 10 percent tithe added*

c. *To help your children practice learning their numbers*

d. *All of the above*

Answers: 1: d, 2: d, 3: c and d—Until your nap is over, which could also be when the Lord returns; 4: b, 5: a and d, 6: d, 7: a and d, 8: d, 9: d, 10: c, 11: d, 12: d

After God created the world, he made man and woman. Then, to keep the whole thing from collapsing, he invented humor.

Guillermo Mordillo

"I'll Be Right Back"

Do not take life too seriously. You will never get out of it alive.
Elbert Hubbard

In 2002, the news covered a story about a Massachusetts doctor who apparently abandoned his patient on the operating table while he left to go cash a check at a nearby bank. His astute reasoning told him that the bank was going to close before the operation would be over, leaving him with no other choice than to leave the patient open so he could catch the bank while it was still open. The patient, of course, was unaware of his doctor's absence during this time, which seems grossly unfair to us. The least the doctor could have done was wake the patient up and ask if he wanted him to pick up a mocha Frappuccino for him while he was out.

The doctor had his medical license yanked because of the incident. Apparently, you can't slip off and do your banking while someone is waiting for you to finish their spinal fusion. It also makes you wonder how many errands your own doctor has run while you were under anesthesia. Do doctors have some sort of chart, letting them know the time frame involved and exactly what sort of things they might be able to get done while we're under? Something along the lines of:

Tonsillectomy? Take clothes to cleaners
Appendectomy? Walk the dog
Cyst removal? Get oil change in car
Gall bladder removal? Return books to library
Pacemaker insertion? Pick up prescription at pharmacy
Repair torn ligament? Get car washed

We're being facetious here, of course. Thankfully most doctors don't take off while their patients are under anesthesia. They know the risks involved and are responsible. But we also know that medical care has become a source of stress for many of us, and it doesn't help to read about situations like the banking doctor and these other actual medical records dictated by physicians:

By the time he was admitted, his rapid heart had stopped, and he was feeling better.

Patient has chest pain if she lies on her left side for over a year.

On the second day the knee was better and on the third day it had completely disappeared.

The patient refused an autopsy.

The patient's past medical history has been remarkably insignificant with only a forty-pound weight gain in the past three days.

In 2003, a Miami judge ordered the Veterans Administration to pay a former patient and his wife $455,000 in damages. Seems a doctor left a sixteen-by-twenty-eight-inch blue cotton surgical towel inside the unsuspecting patient. The medical team knew from CT scans that he had a "foreign object" in his abdomen but discharged him and didn't tell him for three months. (Apparently, they hadn't needed the towel until then.)

Not only do stories like these make us a little nervous about our medical care, but insurance premiums to pay for surgeries and other medical procedures (whether your doctor is out cashing a check or not) are going through the roof. Even in countries like Canada, where there is a national health-care system, the wait and quality of care isn't always as good as it could be. (Phil has been in a Canadian emergency room since the fourth grade waiting to have a hair trasplant.)

For years, society has been working to improve some of our most common complaints. To help alleviate some of the workload on doctors, nursing stations and urgent care offices have now started opening up in pharmacies. That's right, you can now go to the drugstore and see your doctor at the same time. We think this is a great idea. There's nothing like the convenience of having your gallstones removed and being able to get them gift wrapped all in the same place.

As convenient as medical care is getting now, it still stands to reason that if you're going to be operated on, most of us would like the doctor to stick around until we're put back together again. It just seems like the more polite thing to do.

Thanks to modern medicine we are no longer forced to endure prolonged pain, disease, discomfort, and wealth.
Robert Orben

We cannot learn without pain.
Aristotle

Hard to Swallow

Some things that we're faced with both in our refrigerators and in life are simply just hard to swallow. Like the price of gasoline these days. But again, it's all in how you look at it. Believe it or not, there are even some advantages to this hard-to-swallow reality of today's world.

The Blessings of Rising Gas Prices

Don't just sit there complaining about the rising price of gas. Look at the hidden blessings that come along with those prices. Here are just ten of them; we're sure you can think of more:

1. *We've been practicing riding stationary bikes for years in our basements and at our gyms. Now we finally might have the incentive to actually get outside and do it for real.*

2. *Fewer Hummers and SUVs to have to maneuver around in a parking lot.*

3. *Instead of planning that cross-country road trip, we can now*

finally visit that local campground that almost had to close its doors last summer.

4. We can turn the abandoned parking lots into tennis courts.
5. We can walk to work every Monday. Get there by Friday.
6. High gas prices are the perfect excuse to avoid the in-laws.
7. No more teenagers cruising the boulevards on the weekends.
8. No matter where we're from, it gives us all something in common to talk about, besides the weather.
9. Parents don't complain about their teenagers skateboarding anymore.
10. We keep the mileage down on our vehicles.

PART FOUR

Empty Shelves

(Overworked, Overstressed, Overwhelmed, and Underappreciated—and That's the Good News)

> I was so depressed that I decided
> to jump from the tenth floor. They sent up a priest.
> He said, "On your mark . . ."
> *Rodney Dangerfield*

Have you ever felt over-appreciated to the point where you'd really like your children to stop thanking you for all your hard work in the kitchen, at your job, at their schools or sports teams, at church, or wherever else you find yourself working? Have you ever felt way too rested? Or way too overpaid? We suspect not. Very few of us have ever taken a check back to our bosses and said, "I'm sorry, there must be some mistake. I can get by on way less than this." Nor have we said to our spouse or children, "You don't have to thank me. Seeing your clothes strewn all over the floor is thanks enough, sweetie."

If you've ever opened the fridge door and the light wouldn't come on, you know that all things at some point reach their limit of endurance. You have a few choices when this happens. You can remove the light bulb, then lick your finger and stick it into the socket to see if there's any power left.[1] You can chip the dried chocolate pudding out of the light switch until it works again. Or you can remove the light bulb and calmly insert another one. We recommend the third step.[2] Then we recommend that you sit down, remove your shoes, and read the

---

[1] This was a joke. Please do not do this. If you do and there is a problem, please write us at You Did What? Box 403, Lower Zimbabwe.

[2] Some opt for just closing the door and going back to bed.

following tips and stories for the over-stressed, underpaid, and underappreciated who are having trouble seeing the light even when the fridge door is open.

The Stress Diet

Breakfast

1 slice multi-grain toast (lightly buttered)
1 orange (lightly squeezed)
1 cup bran cereal (no sugar)
6 oz. skim milk

Mid-morning

8 oz. iced tea

Lunch

6 oz. lean chicken
Leaf of lettuce, small
8 oz. water, no lemon
Small cluster of grapes
Small scoop of ice cream

Mid-afternoon snack

Mix handful of peanuts, pound of fudge, and a box of chocolates into remaining ice cream. Finish carton.

Dinner

1 large pizza (loaded) with extra cheese
1 medium pan lasagna
Gallon of root beer
2 slices raspberry cheesecake (eat with your hands)
More pizza (eat with your hands)
More ice cream (eat with your face)

Bedtime snack

3 packages of Rolaids[3]
8 tablespoons Pepto Bismol[4]

If people concentrated on the really important things in life, there'd be a shortage of fishing poles.
Doug Larson

---

[3]This is a joke.
[4]This is also a joke.

Choose Your Rut Carefully

I don't know the key to success,
but the key to failure is trying to please everybody.
Bill Cosby

We love reading road signs. Like the one welcoming you to Kettle Falls, Washington, the home of "1,255 friendly people and one grouch." In Hilt, California, a sign advises: "Brakeless trucks, use freeway." Along Oregon's winding coast, another sign warns: "Emergency stopping only. Whale watching is not an emergency. Keep driving." There's a service station somewhere with a bold sign proclaiming, "We have Mexican food. We have gas." While traveling through Kentucky, I (Martha) once saw a traffic warning sign by a construction site on the interstate that said, "Whoa!" and the next one said, "Leave the racing to the horses!" But our favorite of them all is posted on an Alaska highway: "Choose your rut carefully. You'll be in it for the next two hundred miles."

Have you noticed that when you're rushing to get to your destination, you hardly notice any road signs? You're so focused on arriving that the journey becomes more of a blur than a trip. You ate, but you don't really remember where. You stopped for gas but couldn't say which town you were in. You saw an accident, but if anyone was injured, you wouldn't know it because all you could do was complain about the traffic jam it caused.

Rushing also causes us to make more mistakes. We miss our exit and don't realize it until we're twenty-six miles down the road. We can't stop to check out that funny noise our engine is making until we have to stop because the funny noise has left us stranded by the side of the road on I-40. Or we race down the street only to hit every red light possible.

But rushing isn't only done on our highways and streets. It's also done in our homes.

As a young father, I (yes, Phil) found myself in the rut of spending sixty hours at work each week, speaking across the country on weekends, and wallpapering the house at night. I had three small children and one wife, and I was in danger of getting their names mixed up. I was in danger of not just writing about the grouch of Kettle Falls but becoming him, as well. Like the wallpaper, things were about to come crashing down. Before I knew what hit me, I was flat on my back. Burned out. Finished. Kaput.

What happened? I was reading signs. But I was reading all the wrong ones, like, "Give your kids the stuff you never had," "Sign them up for all the extracurricular activities that all your friends have their kids in," and the most dangerous sign of all, "Dads don't really matter. Mom's got it all under control." I was stuck in the rut of believing that an ultra-busy schedule equals a productive and healthy family life. To me, a well-balanced life meant a well-balanced checkbook. If I had enough money for everything my kids wanted and all the sports and arts that they were involved in, then we were successful.

I (Martha) was in the rut of reading signs like, "If you never leave your rut, the road will be smooth." But sometimes even the ruts are a little bumpy. Sometimes they even break way and leave you buried in the snow. It's part of the nature of ruts.

But three liberating truths have freed us from trying to live up to everyone else's expectations or from stressing out over the rocky places of life. We think these three truths should be clearly posted as road signs along life's highway, ruts and all.

1. The fruit of the Spirit is not sour grapes.

In the midst of my (Phil's) burnout, my four-year-old pounced on me and tickled me. I didn't move. "Dad," he said, "you don't laugh so good anymore." I wanted to say that it was because he had landed on my spleen and I was having difficulty breathing, much less laughing. But I knew it was more than that. That night I made a conscious decision to change. I began renting funny, wholesome movies. I bought a few cartoon books and explained the jokes to the kids. Within days, the difference in our home was noticeable. God is a God of joy. He has given us a built-in escape hatch for the pressures of life. It is our funny bone. Laughter has no MSG, no fat grams, no carbs, no trans fat. Laughter is low in cholesterol, and it tastes better than most health food. It's our secret weapon against whatever "sour grapes" life happens to throw at us.

2. Even ants have time to attend picnics.

Recently my (Phil's) family bought a puppy. Mojo cost us three hundred dollars, or a hundred dollars per brain cell. Sometimes she curls up on my lap, her tiny heart beating faster than you'd believe. But when she drifts off to sleep, it slows down remarkably. They say the jumping mouse's heart beats five hundred times a minute. During hibernation, however, it slows to thirty beats per minute. We're not recommending hibernation (although the idea is compelling if we don't meet this deadline), but we are recommending rest. The Bible tells us that Jesus often took a break. No one in history accomplished more than he did, yet he did it all without overworking himself and acquiring an ulcer. Rest allows us to recharge our batteries and reorganize our priorities. The Creator of the universe took time to rest. So should we.

3. Even full shelves sometimes mold.

Read enough road signs and you can't miss the message that you don't have enough. "You don't drive a green Jaguar like this one. You poor soul. How have you lived this long without it? You don't eat glazed ham in a perfect dining room with perfect lighting and the perfect family who laugh at all your jokes while the yellow Lab retriever lies at your feet flea-less and grinning. You call that a life?"

If the rat race is getting you down, here's an exercise you may want to try: Leave your credit cards at home and stroll through a mall laughing at all the things you do not need. We each have done this and enjoyed ourselves immensely. Here are some of the things we've found:

> *A water fountain for your cat*
> *A cell phone that works underwater (thank God for that!)*
> *Alarm clocks[1] that project the time on your ceiling in the middle of the night (when you should be sleeping) but can't be read during the daylight (when you should be getting up)*
> *Gas-powered blenders for the backyard*
> *Pants that talk (they say "Zip me!")*

We don't drive green Jaguars[2] or have perfect families (and the ham on our tables is more burnt than glazed), but we do have some things you can't buy at Wal-Mart. We have a thousand memories we hope to recall in the old-folks' home. We have close, faithful friends who gather round when times get tough.

---

[1] This beauty should be called The Insomniac's Dream
[2] Though Martha has part of one on her bumper from a parking lot incident.

We have enough money to give some of it away. And when we notice that the neighbor's grass is greener, we remind ourselves that their water bill is probably higher. And, oh yes, they have to cut it more often, too.

I try to take one day at a time,
but sometimes several days attack me at once.
Jenifer Yane

I have learned from experience that
the greater part of our happiness or misery depends
on our dispositions and not on our circumstances.
Martha Washington

Not So Smooth Moves

It's a funny thing being a writer. During those terrifying moments in life when you know you are going to die, whether at the hands of a stubborn parachute, a leaky canoe, or your mother-in-law's wild driving, all you can think of is: I sure hope I live so I can write about this! But there are also those horrifying occasions when you have done something so incredibly dumb that you know you will never have the courage to confess it to your faithful and long-suffering readers.

Knowing, however, that our readers are above average and can keep a secret, we have decided to confess several of the dumbest things we have managed to accomplish over the years.

First off, we want you to know that we are not alone. Others have accomplished similar dim-witted deeds. We'd feel better if we exposed them first.

A Wisconsin man makes us feel much better. Before leaving on vacation, he decided he should hide his handguns and ammunition, just in case thieves broke in and stole them. But where do you hide such things? In the oven, of course. Who would ever look in an oven for artillery? Unfortunately he forgot to tell his wife where he'd placed them, and when they got home from vacation, well, you can guess the rest. Turning on the oven to cook dinner, she got the surprise of her life. *USA Today* reported that when the bullets began exploding, the couple took cover behind their refrigerator. Finally the intrepid husband was able to use an extinguisher to put out the fire (and firearms). Luckily no one got hurt, but I guess that's one way to put a hole in your Bundt cake!

In Great Britain, a truck driver by the name of Klaus Buergermeister ran into a Smart car without knowing he had. Klaus proceeded to drive for two miles with the tiny vehicle wedged to the front of his semi, before being flagged down by police. (I know Alabama truck drivers have hit some pretty good-sized mosquitoes, but nothing like this.) Andreas Bolga, the terrified driver of the so-called Smart car, was finally able to escape before anything worse happened. Klaus, age fifty-three, told *The Express* newspaper that he had felt only a slight bump and added: "I could not believe it when I got out and saw there was a car stuck on the front of my truck."

At the pinnacle of my (Phil's) hockey career, as all the teenage girls in our little town watched, I scored the overtime goal of the championship game! Quite a feat. Except that I scored it into my own net. I was publicly humiliated, to say the least. In fact, I don't remember much about the next eight or ten years of my life. But I do remember what happened when I got home after the game. My father sat with me, and he grinned. Then he snickered. Then he laughed with me. And best of all he told me he loved me in spite of my very public mistake.

I (Martha) have shared this story before, but it bears repeating. Once while in one of those super shoe stores, I decided to try on a pair of boots. I looked around for a place to sit down, but all the stools were taken. Behind me, however, was a row of large boxes that obviously dozens of shoes were shipped in. I figured I would just turn around and take a seat on one of those.

My plan would have worked had the boxes had anything in them, but because they were *empty,* when I sat down, I sank all the way to the floor. My legs were now sticking up out of the box like a couple of chopsticks in a Chinese takeout meal. It was a tight fit and I couldn't budge. So I had to rock the box side to side to get it to fall over so I could crawl out! Since this store was at the mall, there's no telling how many people were watching from the window.[1]

The embarrassing moments of life are good reminders that it's good to be humbled. Humility. It's the one thing few of us ask God for, but it's so necessary in life. Humility keeps us from judging others too harshly. It also reminds us that we have a Father who smiles and sometimes even laughs with us in the midst of our dumbest mistakes. Why? Because he has an eternal perspective, and because he knows we're not perfect. And if we're wise, we'll learn from those mistakes.

We're sure that Wisconsin couple has learned and by now must have found a regular cooking timer instead of their Smith & Wessons. And we're sure that truck driver probably checks his bumper for small cars every time he stops now.

And now when Martha tries on shoes, she makes sure the seat where she sits isn't a trapdoor. As for Phil's new hockey career? Well, whenever he plays now, the sign his team has hung above the opposing net that says "THIS ONE!" has sure helped a lot!

---

[1] If you were there and had been wondering all these years who the chopstick lady was, now you know.

Finish each day and be done with it.
You have done what you could; some blunders and absurdities
have crept in; forget them as soon as you can. Tomorrow is a
new day; you shall begin it serenely and with too high a spirit to
be encumbered with your old nonsense.

Ralph Waldo Emerson

High Hopes

Blessed is he who expects nothing
for he shall never be disappointed.
Alexander Pope

We're sure this has happened to you. You're craving that last
piece of chocolate cream pie. You saw it in the refrigerator just
this morning and have been putting off eating it until now. After
all, you couldn't very well have it for breakfast. Chocolate cream
pie isn't a breakfast food, at least not in the same way that pizza
is. You didn't even have it for lunch, because that's the meal
you've been trying to cut back on and just have a health drink.
But now it's dinnertime. You had only a salad, passing up the
mashed potatoes and dinner rolls just so you could indulge in
this one pleasure—the last piece of chocolate cream pie! You have
been surprisingly disciplined, passing when the pie first made its
go-around. You've been good. But now there's only one piece left
and you've staked your claim on it. You didn't shove a flag into
the whipped cream or anything like that to claim it. But you have

made it known to the entire family that the last piece of pie is yours.

You've excused yourself from the table and walked to the refrigerator, fork in hand. You're not even going to dirty another plate. You'll just eat it right out of the pie tin. You open the fridge door and what do you see? Cheese, butter, eggs, six jars of jelly, some leftover pot roast, but no pie! What happened to your pie?! You turn to ask your beloved family, the family you work forty-eight hours a day for. The spouse you pledged your love to. The children you birthed. Even your mother-in-law. But no one is 'fessing up. At least not at first. Then your three-year-old confesses. You're impressed with her honesty, but that was *your* piece of pie. She was the only one you hadn't been emphatic with. You didn't think you needed to be because she can't even open the refrigerator, right? Apparently she can, and apparently she and the dog enjoyed your piece of chocolate cream pie together. You know this because of the whipped cream you find in the dog's ear.

Disappointment. Life is full of it. Being denied your piece of pie is sad, but there are far sadder stories that have to do with disappointment.

A second grader watches as everyone else in the class gets Valentine's cards, but his bag remains empty.

A bride gets left at the altar.

An old man gets dressed up for his birthday and waits all day for someone to show up to celebrate it with him, but no one comes.

Disappointment can sure rob us of our joy, can't it? What hurts so much about disappointment is the negative self-talk we go through after it:

"Why'd I get my hopes up, anyway? I should know by now that nothing goes right for me."

"Of course no one gave me a Valentine. Who'd give me one?"

"I should have known I'd get passed over for that promotion. What was I thinking to even apply for it?"

What makes disappointment so bad is the gnawing notion inside of us that says we wouldn't have had so far to fall if we hadn't built up our expectations so high in the first place. If we hadn't even tried out for *American Idol,* we wouldn't have known what it feels like to be rejected. If we hadn't told everyone we know about that new house we were going to buy, we wouldn't be so embarrassed now that the loan didn't go through. If we hadn't told them we loved them, it wouldn't hurt so much to hear them say they don't love us back.

Disappointment.

But even disappointment can be a good thing. I (Martha) remember one of the toughest afternoons of my life happening when one of the "cool kids" at my junior high school invited me to a party. She gave me her phone number and told me to call and find out where it was going to be. But later that night when I went to call, I couldn't find that phone number anywhere. I remember looking all over the house and crying, feeling like my big chance was passing me by.

My mother was sympathetic, but looking back I wonder if she also hadn't protectively "misplaced" the number herself. This was back in the sixties, and a party with a bunch of teenagers that she didn't know probably wasn't her idea of a safe environment. My mother is gone now, so I'll probably never know what really happened to that phone number. I do know, however, that I got over my disappointment and went on with my life. I also found out the next day that the party had turned into something I wouldn't have wanted to be at anyway.

There's a wonderful old poem written by Edith Lillian Young. Think through the words carefully:

Disappointment—His Appointment
Change one letter, then I see
That the thwarting of my purpose
Is God's better choice for me.
His appointment must be blessing,
Tho' it may come in disguise,
For the end from the beginning
Open to His wisdom lies.[1]

Disappointment . . . sometimes it's for our own good. But now, being cheated out of the last piece of a chocolate pie? Well, that's just too sad for words!

Disappointment is the nurse of wisdom.
Boyle Roche

---

[1]Public domain.

Sometimes the Answer Is Right in Front of You

When one door of happiness closes, another opens;
but often we look so long at the closed door that we
do not see the one which has been opened for us.

Helen Keller

Have you ever stood staring into the fridge wondering, *Where on earth is the blue cheese dressing?*[1] To make matters worse, someone else comes along, looks over your shoulder, and says, "It's right there beside the milk. Are you blind?"

We heard a story about a young boy named Pedro who kept riding his bicycle across the border between Mexico and America, lugging two bags on his shoulders. Every day the border patrol would stop Pedro to ask him what was in his bags. Pedro would say "sand," and they would still make him empty the bags onto

---

[1]We have also stood staring into the fridge wondering what we're doing there. Martha once put a dish rag in the fridge while she was cleaning up. Phil put ice cream in the fridge, then after it melted, refroze it. His children were teenagers. They thought it tasted fine.

the ground to prove it. But Pedro wasn't lying. The bags were filled with sand.

The next day Pedro would ride across the border again, and again the border patrol would stop him.

"What's in your bags?" they would ask.

"Sand," Pedro would answer.

"Prove it," they'd say. So Pedro would dump out both bags and show them the sand. Once they were satisfied, Pedro would scoop up the sand in his hands and put it all back into his bags. This daily routine went on for six months, with Pedro peddling across the border and the border patrol stopping him and making him empty his bags.

Then one day Pedro didn't show up. The border patrol wondered what happened to the young man with the bags, but they continued with their inspections. Months passed, and finally one of the border patrol officers happened to run into Pedro in town.

"Pedro! How have you been?" he said.

"Fine," answered Pedro.

Then the officer said, "Pedro, we know you were smuggling something across the border every day. Come on, you can tell me, what was it?"

Pedro smiled and said, "Bicycles."

Sometimes, when we look back, things are so obvious. The next chapter reminds us of something we're often too busy to discover, a last resort that should come first.

Never miss a good chance to shut up.
Will Rogers

Who Ya Gonna Call?

*Whether you like it or no, read and pray daily. It is for your life;
there is no other way; else you will be a trifler all your days.*

John Wesley

When I (Phil) was a little kid, my mother prayed for me every
night. I would walk by her bedroom and see her by her bed,
down on her knees. Once I crept up close enough to overhear
her. "Oh, thank you, God, he's finally in bed!"

According to recent surveys conducted by legitimate compa-
nies who have the postage for this sort of thing, the vast majority
of us believe in prayer, and most of us would agree that God does
indeed answer prayer. Sometimes his answer is no, as in the case
of my new bass boat request, or Martha's trip to London, but he
does answer.

Can you imagine what this world would be like if God gave us
everything we asked of him? Little brothers the world over would
never see their tenth birthday because sisters would have prayed
for God to return their annoying sibling back to where he came

from. And he would have done it. At least in a world where God gave us everything we asked for.

And remember in third grade when you prayed, "Lord, I just really really want that cute new boy to like me and to really really want to grow up and marry me. Oh, pulleeeze, please, please, please! I won't ask you for another thing ever again! If you loved me, God, you would do this!" And there you would be, engaged in the third grade to some guy whom you would pray about in the fourth grade: "Lord, that new boy turned out to be such a jerk! I hate him, God! I don't even want him sitting next to me, much less to grow up and marry me! He's so immature! That noise he makes with his armpit drives me right up a wall! If he thinks I'm going to live with that the rest of my life, he's got another think coming! If you loved me, God, you'd just make him go away!" Then in the twelfth grade, "Maybe I was acting a bit hasty, Lord. That new boy turned out to be pretty nice after all. And cute! I know you did what I asked and he hasn't been in a single class of mine since, but could you back off on that request and put him in one now? And maybe even have him sit next to me. And ask me out. Pulleeeze, please, please, please! I know he still makes that awful noise with his armpit, but I think I can live with it now! If you loved me, God, you'd do this for me!" Then, after five years of marriage, "What kind of a jerk did you stick me with, God? I know I begged for you to make him love me, but there's this other cute guy I met the other night, and I really would like to get to know him better, and I know I made a commitment, but if you really, really loved me . . ."

It's a good thing God doesn't answer all our prayers. And what about all those promises we make to him?

"Lord, if you just give me this one thing, I will serve you in the most remote corner of the rain forest."

God says, "You're not even serving me now."

"Well, sure, that's now. But give me my request and you'll see how much I'll do for you."

So God gives us our request and he does see. He sees the closest we get to the rain forest is watching a special on the Travel channel.

When I (Martha) was a teenager, I remember praying for a guitar one Christmas. I wanted that guitar more than anything else in the world. I hinted to my parents, I even showed them the exact one I wanted every time we went to the store. But on Christmas morning, there wasn't a guitar-shaped gift under the Christmas tree. I tried to act excited about my other gifts, but I had really wanted that guitar, and it was hard to talk myself out of the disappointment. But then my mother took me into one of the bedrooms, and there in the corner was my guitar. It wasn't wrapped. It was just leaning against the wall. I couldn't believe it! I had gotten my guitar! I was so excited I don't think I put that guitar down the entire day! After that, I don't think I picked it up. I never did learn to play that guitar. I had begged for it, prayed for it, dreamed about it, but when I got it, I just let it sit there and gather dust.

How many times have we done that with God? We've prayed, "Lord, if you'll just give me this opportunity to use my talents or bless me with the job of my dreams, I'll do this for you or that for you," and when God does his part, we forget all about our promises. We just move on to the next request.

And amazingly enough, he keeps listening. That's because it's his nature. Our natural tendency is to let him down. His is to be faithful. Ours is to selfishly ask for things we don't really need. His is to love us enough not to give us everything we want. Our nature is to complain about the place where we find ourselves. His is to know that what we're going through is for our own good and to protect us through it but never lose sight of the goal.

Back in 2003, a most unusual event took place up in Canada,

where Phil lives. Called the Heritage Classic, it was an outdoor hockey game featuring the Edmonton Oilers and the Montreal Canadiens. When the NHL announced plans for the game to be held in snowy Edmonton in cold November, most fans had one thought on their minds: *What? Are you crazy? Who will come? It will be minus-thirty-five degrees by game time!* But they were wrong. It was only minus twenty. And the fans showed up in droves. More than fifty-five thousand fans jammed Commonwealth Stadium to watch their heroes play. More surprising still was that the team received almost one million requests for tickets!

Rumor has it that one lady called the box office and was told the tickets were sold out. So she called the city of Edmonton. They directed her to the Edmonton Oilers hockey team. When she called the team, she was turned down once again. So she decided to call her son.

"Wayne," she said, "is there some way you can get me tickets for the game?"

"Of course, Mother," said Wayne Gretzky. "It's no problem."

Whether the story is true or not, we do not know. But this we do know. Talking to God is so often the last resort for many of us. We do the same thing as Mrs. Gretzky. We wait until we have no other recourse, no other place to turn. But it shouldn't be that way. Prayer should be the first place we turn.

Prayer can do a lot of things. It can alter our circumstances and "altar" our desire to control them. It can change our hearts. It can change other people's hearts. It can open our eyes. It can open the eyes of those who have hurt us. It can bring healing into our lives.

It can bring us peace. It can bring understanding to misunderstanding. It can bring about a miracle. It tells God how much we trust him. It tells God how much we love him. And it can tell him how much we need him. It's our way of communicating with him. We can talk to him about our frustrations, our fears, our hurts, and our desires. We can ask him questions. We can thank him for what he's already done in our past and for what he's going to do in our future. We can apologize for the times we've failed him. We can receive grace and forgiveness. We can receive strength and direction. Prayer is powerful. And healing. And best of all, free. There are no roaming charges, and we don't have to wait until the weekend to get a better rate.

For I am convinced that neither death nor life,
neither angels nor demons, neither the present nor the future,
nor any powers, neither height nor depth, nor anything else
in all creation, will be able to separate us from
the love of God that is in Christ Jesus our Lord.
Romans 8:38–39

Prayer does not change God, but it changes him who prays.
S. A. Kierkegaard

PART FIVE

Just Desserts

(The Best Is Yet to Come)

> To believe in heaven is not to run away from life;
> it is to run toward it.
>
> *Joseph D. Blinco*

There's a church in Tennessee that sits at the end of a road called Little Hope. When I (Martha) first saw the road and the church, I thought, who would want to go to a church on a street named Little Hope? But the more I thought about it, the more I decided that if you ever suddenly found yourself on Little Hope Road, it's probably kind of nice to know there's a church at the end of it.

We all need hope, the belief that something better lies at the end of this struggle. The conviction that what we see around us is not all there is. Hope gives us a reason to keep waking up each morning. To rise when we fail. To smile when the world says frown.

Church has always been a big part of both of our lives. When I (Martha) and my husband went through the ordeal of a stillbirth, the church we were going to at the time became like family. They encouraged us, prayed with us, and were there with open arms offering us friendship and hope during a difficult time in our lives. Our joy turned to three separate celebrations as three sons were added to our family. And our church family was there with open arms once again, to share in each of those celebrations.

When my (Phil's) wife began having seizures and was tested for Huntington's disease, it was friends in our church who cried with us, baby-sat the kids, and even brought casseroles. God's people, who really live for others, give us a tiny foretaste of what heaven will be like, and help provide hope down here.

Hope opens doors that despair has slammed shut. Hope looks for the good instead of camping on the worst. Hope turns problems into opportunities and fear into faith. Here are some stories of hope for the paranoid, the fearful, and those whose fridges are filled with food that has long since passed its expiration dates.

In Case You Haven't Noticed, This Isn't Paradise

**Happiness often sneaks in through a door
you didn't know you left open.**
John Barrymore

If you were one of the lucky ones who was handed a brochure at birth that said, "Welcome to paradise! Get ready to embark on a pain-free, problem-free journey where there will be no main course, only dessert," this chapter isn't for you. You have our permission to skip on ahead. If, however, you're like the rest of us and all you got was a slap on the backside and a disinfectant bath from a nurse named Attila, then you may have a firm grasp of the fact that this world ain't paradise.[1]

In second grade I (Phil) discovered firsthand that this world isn't paradise. Back in those primitive times, they used to line us up alphabetically in the school hallway for a meeting with a huge

---

[1]Please don't write telling us that ain't ain't a word. We already know it ain't.

nurse who wore a name tag that said B. L. We didn't know what the initials stood for, so we called her Big Lump. Some people are kind and good. Some people smile a lot. Not B. L. She was mean. She never smiled. In fact, she looked so sour she could have probably sucked rivets off a skateboard. Thankfully my last name put me at the front of the line, so I didn't have time to be terrified. In one hand Big Lump held a needle the size of barbeque tongs. In her other hand, she balanced the rest of it. I stepped forward, staring at the sword—I mean, needle. She jerked my sleeve up over my tiny shoulder blade, swabbed my skinny little arm, and jammed that shiny needle home. I wasn't sure, but I thought I felt it go out the other side. I hollered loudly. I didn't care what the other students thought. That sucker hurt! Then B. L. handed me a sugar cube to soothe the pain. As if that would help. I didn't care what I was being immunized against, all I remember thinking was that there was no way the disease could have been worse than the precaution. But at least I did find something to be thankful for. I was glad my name wasn't Zaccheus Zabolotney, who stood terrified at the back of that line, waiting his turn, listening to everyone's screams as they filed by.

Whether we have time to prepare for it or not, life gives us pain. It can give us pain even when it's trying to protect us. Believe it or not, it can also give us pain when we're trying to do good.

When my (Martha's) son and daughter-in-law asked if I would feed and walk their six-month-old border collie for them, I said sure. But they had one of those releaseable dog leashes that I wasn't used to operating. I held the leash in my left hand and the control in my right. (I've since learned that the instructions say this is not advisable. I now know why.)

As soon as the dog hit the outdoors she took off, and I could feel the leash zip through the palm of my hand with such force, I was sure that the leash had sliced right through it. I paused briefly to look down at my palm, fully expecting to see a geyser of blood. But it wasn't bleeding. What happened next, however, is all a slow-motion blur. Taking full advantage of my diverted attention, and too excited about seeing a neighbor boy out front to contain her enthusiasm, that dog took off like a bullet, taking me with her. I tried my best to keep up, my legs moving as fast as they possibly could, until I finally gave up and just went with it.

I don't know how long I was airborne. In my memory it seemed about as long as one of Tinkerbell's flights with Peter Pan, but without the grace and fairy dust. When I came back down, I was cheek to cheek with the asphalt street,[2] getting a derma-peel the hard way.[3] My face was scratched and bruised, my knee was scraped and bruised, and my forearms and shoulders had bruises, too. All this from doing a good deed. The dog got his afternoon walk and I got an afternoon flight. But even though I was hurt, I have to say I've laughed more over that incident than I've cried.

Things aren't going to go perfectly for any of us. We were never promised that. But if we look hard enough at our troubles, we can usually find something to laugh about.

And if nothing else, these pains and embarrassments of life can remind us that this may not be paradise. But it's coming.

He will wipe every tear from their eyes. There will be no more death or mourning or crying or pain, for the old order of things has passed away.

Revelation 21:4

You don't stop laughing because you grow old;
you grow old because you stop laughing.

Michael Pritchard

---

[2]Sounds like a country song.
[3]Sounds like a crooner song.

In order to maintain a well-balanced perspective, the person who has a dog to worship him should also have a cat to ignore him.

Peterborough Examiner

Best Before 1983

Don't carry a grudge. While you're carrying the grudge,
the other guy's out dancing.
Buddy Hackett

Expiration dates. Most food products have them. They may be hidden under all the mold that has grown over them, but they're in there somewhere. Even if the expiration date isn't stamped on the packaging, common sense tells us that there is a shelf life to most food products. After a certain amount of time, they're going to lose their nutritional value and perhaps even become harmful to us if eaten.

I (Martha) once uncovered a cucumber in my vegetable drawer that had more moss growing on it than the Swamp Thing. It had obviously lived with me well beyond its "expiration date," which for vegetables is usually somewhere between the time you buy it at the grocery store and the time it petrifies.

Like that cucumber, there are other things that don't have expiration dates printed on them, but they should.

We believe that grudges should have expiration dates. The

hurt is what someone does to us. The grudge is what we do to ourselves, and if we're smart, we'll put an expiration date on it.

Husbands and wives should put expiration dates on some of their disagreements, too. I (Phil) once had a heated argument with my wife days before Christmas. It gave a whole new meaning to "Silent Night." But whether it happened five years ago, ten years ago, or even two hours ago, if it's already been discussed and worked through, let's throw it out like the Swamp Thing cucumber.

Do you know we have expirations dates, too? Each and every one of us. For some of us it might be May 6, 2010. For others it could be December 1, 2014. Or perhaps even December 1 of this year. None of us like thinking about it, but we have an expiration date that only God knows. None of us can avoid it. One hundred percent of people are dying now. It's an epidemic.

Maybe it would have been a good idea if God had stamped an expiration date on our bodies somewhere. Our behavior toward others and toward ourselves might change just a little if we had to look at that expiration date each time we looked in the mirror. We might be more patient with the people around us:

"What an absolute self-centered, egotistical jerk she is! Oh, wait. It says on her forehead that she's due to expire next week. You know, maybe I should cut her a little slack instead. Only God knows what is really going on in her life."

Or "I wish I had more time to spend with my son. But I'm just so busy. Wait, it says here that his expiration date is—I'm not going to the office today. I'm taking my son to the park."

With personal expiration dates, we would probably be a lot more forgiving of others, too.

"Do you have any idea what he did? Well, let me tell you . . .

"Oh, wait. It says here that I'm due to expire this afternoon. Maybe I should go a little lighter on him since God does say that I'm going to be judged in the same way I've judged others. Okay, never mind. Forget I even brought him up. Just pray for him, which is what I guess I should have been doing for him all along anyway."

There's no telling what kind of positive behavior an expiration date might inspire in all of us. If we had a true awareness of how much longer we had, we'd let a lot of things slide. We wouldn't stress over many of the situations that cause us so much anguish now. We would put our attention on the truly important things and not waste our time on things that don't really matter. Who cares if someone is gossiping or lying about us? They've got their own expiration date to worry about. Who cares about that offense that happened ten years ago? Are we going to spend the last five, ten, or fifteen years of our lives fretting over that, or are we going to, like Tim McGraw sings, live like we are dying?

Expiration dates—we can either pay attention and let them move us to action, or we can ignore the big picture and end up throwing away far too many precious years.

> This is the day the Lord has made;
> let us rejoice and be glad in it.
> *Psalm 118:24*

Sweeter Than Honey

All I have seen teaches me to trust
the Creator for all I have not seen.
Ralph Waldo Emerson

Did you know that there is a food that will never spoil? It's honey, a personal favorite of folks like Winnie the Pooh and at least one of us. Other foods will last for years in your refrigerator without so much as a complaint or an explosion. There's molasses, for instance, and baking soda. But for the most part, food that's in there too long will take on a life of it's own, and before long it will turn rotten.[1] But honey is one of those miracle foods.

It's hard to find things on this earth that will not decay.

I (Phil) have three autographed Toronto Blue Jays bats in my basement, given to me after I spoke to the team. You can get on eBay and make some good money with these. The problem is that when my sons were younger, they discovered that these bats were great for hitting rocks and trees . . . and each other.

---

[1]Most of us learn this lesson in a college dormitory.

The bats were priceless once.

Not anymore.

So it is with most of what we see around us. Look out your window now. How much of what you see will last forever? How much of what we're investing our lives in will mold, crack, peel, rust, snap, or wind up in a landfill somewhere?

Next time you open the fridge door and find something growing in there, let it remind you of the things that will never rot, petrify, or corrode. Scripture promises that God's Word and people last forever. And it offers great news about our inheritance:

> *Praise be to the God and Father of our Lord Jesus Christ! In his great mercy he has given us new birth into a living hope through the resurrection of Jesus Christ from the dead, and into an inheritance that can never perish, spoil or fade—kept in heaven for you.*
> *1 Peter 1:3–4*

How sweet is the promise of heaven. It's the assurance that we have an inheritance that outlasts even honey. It's a written guarantee from the only one who hasn't broken a promise yet.

Faith is believing what one cannot see,
and the reward of faith is to see what one believes.
St. Augustine

The Sky Is Always Falling

I read that 75 percent of Americans are now anxious and depressed and I thought, Well, I'm a little ahead of my time, aren't I? The fact is that I have been on a state of high alert since high school. I didn't need 9/11. I was uptight on 9/10.

Garry Shandling, quoted in Servant *magazine*

The Paranoid's Guide to Life

1. If a tree falls in a forest, it'll land on me.
2. A person with the Asian flu will be on my flight, sitting next to me . . . with a screaming, sneezing child on her lap.
3. The chances are excellent that there will be an earthquake today somewhere in the vicinity of where I'm standing.
4. I won the Publisher's Clearing House sweepstakes? That can mean only one thing. I've got two weeks to live.
5. I think I'm being stalked. People are following my every step. I move, they move. I stop, they stop. I've got to get out of this line!

6. An apple a day raises your chances of choking by 400 percent.
7. Everybody hates me, except mosquitoes. And they only use me as a last resort.
8. If I take cover in a storm cellar, a tornado will actually form inside it.
9. The only thing we have to fear is . . . where do I start?
10. A bird in the hand will mean a bite in the palm. Or worse.
11. The best laid plans of mice and men will both be better than mine.
12. I finally have a day off to go to the beach. A tsunami must be coming.
13. This is the first day of the rest of my disasters.

But We Don't Have to Live in Fear

Fear is static that prevents me from hearing myself.
Samuel Butler

People are built to handle varying degrees of worry. First, there are the ones who worry about everything. The Chicken Littles. They run around telling the world that the sky is falling. They worry about the stock market crashing, World War III breaking out, Y3K, California falling into the ocean after a ten-point earthquake, rare virus outbreaks, and any number of other calamities befalling the world's population. Not that those things can't or won't happen,[1] but the possibility of their happening in the future can dominate our present, if we let it.

Then there are the people on the other end of the spectrum. The daredevils. The Evel Knievels of this world who don't lose a minute of sleep over anything. If the sky starts to fall, they'll just open their umbrella and go on about their day. They'll buy property right on top of an earthquake fault or at the base of a

---

[1] If you're paranoid, we wish to point out that they likely will happen on Wednesday, May 3.

volcano. There are some people who will even go on tornado chasing tours.[2] That's right, these people pay someone to drive them *to* a tornado. Now, when it comes to tornadoes, *to* isn't the direction we would recommend. *Away* seems like it would be a much better trip. Don't get us wrong. We're not saying you have to be a worrywart, or a Chicken Little for that matter, but when it comes to your personal safety, we just feel it's best to use common sense and balance. Don't be extreme in either direction. Don't picnic by an alligator-infested swamp, even if it is the Fourth of July and it's the last picnic table available. But don't hide out in your house worrying about a giant mosquito swooping you up the minute you step outside, either. Unless you live in Alabama.

To help you know what is appropriate to stress over and what isn't (for instance, funnel clouds are a justified stress, funnel cakes aren't), we have provided the following list:

Justified Stress:
  Global warming
  Natural disasters
  Getting mugged
  Losing a job
  Bullies
  A shopping cart totaling your parked car (given the right wind conditions, it could happen)

Things Not to Fear:
  All of the above

Why? The explanation is found in Isaiah 26:3: "You will keep in perfect peace him whose mind is steadfast, because he trusts in you."

––––––––––––

[2]Exhibit A: The film *Twister*.

Top Ten Fears

According to people who research these kinds of things, the top ten fears are:

10. *Dogs*
 9. *Loneliness*
 8. *Flying*
 7. *Death*
 6. *Sickness*
 5. *Deep water*
 4. *Financial problems*
 3. *Insects and bugs*
 2. *Heights*
 1. *Public speaking*

Did you notice that the number one fear isn't death? It's public speaking. Public speaking has caused death (for both the speaker, if he's nervous, and for the audience, if he's boring), but we personally find it interesting that on a list of fears, it's number one and death is number seven. People would rather rest in the casket than be the one to read the eulogy. But let's take a look at these fears and examine each one a little more closely.

Dogs. Sure, they can bite, but can they drive? If you're stressing over getting bitten by some ferocious pitbull, look on the positive side. Yes, the dog could very well bite your leg off, but can he drive a car and track you down? Of course not. So calm down. You never have to worry about getting hit by a car being driven by a dog, except in Walt Disney movies. Now, doesn't that make you feel better already?

Loneliness. Is it really all that bad? To feel better about your loneliness, imagine yourself opening your door to unexpected company that includes three toddlers and a teenage punk rocker who brought along his electric guitar. Still feel lonely? Still longing for "a little company"? Or does your peace and quiet suddenly look bearable?

Flying. I (Martha) once sat next to a teenager on her very first flight. She was pretty apprehensive, but I think it was mainly the result of not knowing what to expect. As the plane began to taxi its way toward the runway, she turned to me and asked, "Do the wings flap when we take off?" Fear of the unknown can be a terrible thing. But when it comes to flying, if you focus on everything that will be happening once you get to your destination (reconnecting with loved ones, the vacation of a lifetime, business opportunities, or just a weekend of fun at a place you've always wanted to go), it'll make the flight seem that much more enjoyable and speedy. And for those of you who really don't know, to answer the question, no, the wings don't flap when you take off. If they ever do, make them stop the plane and then go choose a different airline.

Death. Sure, it's a reality, but since we don't know those expiration dates we talked about, none of us really knows where or when it's going to happen, do we? I wonder how many people are still walking around today who thought twenty years ago they were a goner. Don't waste your life worrying about your death. When it happens, you'll be the first one to know.

Sickness. Even if we take all the precautions possible (wear surgical masks, stay away from people, sterilize our dishes four or five times), we can still get sick. Sure, it's wise not to put ourselves in situations where we are exposed unnecessarily to germs. But we don't have to hide away in our basements trying to escape from them, either. Again, a happy balance is the best. If you're still not sure, skip back a few pages to The Paranoid's Guide to Life.

Deep water. Do you know you can drown in shallow water just as easily as you can drown in deep water? All it takes is for water to fill your lungs, and that can happen if you're lying face-down by the steps of the kiddie pool as well as in the twelve-foot-deep section. I (Martha) had a near drowning experience once. (I know I'm blond, but it wasn't because I couldn't shut off the drinking fountain.) It was a real drowning experience, so water is a fear of mine. But I admit that sometimes it's an irrational fear. The "No Lifeguard" sign over my bathtub is probably taking things a little too far. (Yes, I really do have one.)

Financial problems. They say the number one thing that couples fight about is money. Usually it's the lack of it, but believe it or not, in some instances it's the abundance of it. If you don't think too much money can be a problem, just follow an estate dispute after some rich relative dies. People who have been close since birth will suddenly not speak to one another for the rest of their lives—over what? Uncle Buford's double-wide trailer and his forty shares of Studebaker stock?

The apostle Paul warned us about this attitude when he said that he had learned to be content in all things. He said, "I know what it is to be in need, and I know what it is to have plenty. I have learned the secret of being content in any and every situation, whether well fed or hungry, whether living in plenty or in want" (Philippians 4:12). In other words, if you have the money to cruise the Mediterranean this summer, be content. If all you can afford is a pedal-boat ride at a local amusement center, be content. If you're living in a mansion, be content. If you're sleeping in the broom closet at work, be content. If you're eating steak and lobster, be content. If you're eating corn dogs and goldfish crackers, be content. Those who have learned to adjust to their circumstances are the ones who won't break when the going gets tough and the money gets going.

Insects and bugs. Sure, bugs are icky. No one likes to put their feet under a blanket and find a daddy longlegs down there waiting to jump on you. But do insects and bugs really deserve the power we've given them? Let's face it, we're a whole lot bigger than they are. They're the ones who should be fearing us. But do they? Seriously, do they? No, they laugh at us. They see us cowering behind the sofa whenever we see one of them up in the corner of our ceiling. They're at least eight feet away from us and we're frozen in fear. They hear us screaming for our spouse to bring us a shoe, a board, or some other "weapon," and you know they've got to be laughing their little opisthosomata off over all of this drama. We can easily step on these creatures, we can flatten them in less than a second, yet the very thought of them keeps us up at night and has us paying a hundred dollars every three months for an exterminator to come to our home and spray poison all over our baseboards (poison that we ourselves have to leave the house for). Does this make any sense? We even cringe looking at dead insects. What happened to our courage, people? Our ancestors used to sleep out in the desert on rocks. Who knows what kind of critters crawled across their faces in the middle of the night. But did they run and hide? Did they scream for their spouses to wake up and save them? Of course not. And don't even get us started on flying insects. A single bee can get us running faster than an Olympic gold medalist. One wasp flying around outside our car will have us rolling up the windows and locking the doors like it was some kind of serial killer. And if it's on our windshields, the closest we'll get to it is our windshield wipers. How silly we must look to these creatures. When are we going to quit allowing them to control us? When are we going to stand up and finally show some courage? And when is someone going to come in here and kill that spider in the corner of the office that we've had our eye on for the last twenty minutes?

Heights. If this is the world's number two fear, then that means there are plenty of us walking around on the bottom floor of most buildings. But are heights really something to be feared? As tall people, we can tell you that being a little higher than so many others isn't all that scary. Sure, the air's a little thinner, and when we trip and fall, we have a little farther to go than the rest of you, but other than that, there's really nothing to fear. Except, of course, shopping for pants.

And finally, the number one fear—**public speaking.** This is the biggie. But as public speakers, we can tell you unequivocally that this fear *is* justified. It *is* scary going on stage in front of a group of people and talking. You'll start hyperventilating and breaking out into a cold sweat, and you'll feel like you're about to pass out. And that's just if you're announcing the main speaker. We both have tried all the tricks. We've pictured the audience in their underwear. That gave us nightmares for months. We've tried pinching our wrists. That just gave us bruises. We've taken deep breaths. That made us dizzy. Public speaking is a real fear to be dealt with, and there's no getting around it. But now, if you're speaking in a conference room at the top of the Empire State Building and there's a spider in the corner and you're afraid you're going to get stuck with the luncheon tab, and suddenly the fire sprinklers come on and the room fills up with deep water, and you catch a bad cold and have to be flown to a hospital and kept in isolation where you're all by yourself (except for the hospital pit bull they let visit you every morning) until you die, well, nothing we say here could even help you then.

Fear only two: God and the man who has no fear of God.
Hasidic saying

Leftovers

If your refrigerator is like ours, it's probably full of leftovers. There will be containers of leftover Chinese food, a single slice of pizza in a pizza box that someone has laid on top of a plastic container of leftover meatloaf and mashed potatoes that now appear to be glowing, a gallon carton with enough milk left in it for a single cup of coffee, six jars of jelly, one ketchup bottle turned upside down so that the four drops left in it will come out more easily, and cheese that has marbled into some kind of moldy sculpture. Not a very appetizing mix, but then, leftovers seldom are as good as the original.

Have you ever known someone who thought all they deserved is leftovers? They wait until everyone is finished with their meal, and then they proceed to eat off all the plates? Even though there is plenty of food available in the serving dishes, they are more than content to simply finish what others have left behind.

We both strongly believe that God has a plan for each one of our lives, and it is a whole lot better than other people's leftovers. But too often we settle. Those leftovers are so much easier to reach.

It's like comparing the cookie dough in the freezer with the half-eaten cookie on the table. The one on the table is easier to grab. And it involves no work on our part. We don't have to bake it or frost it or do anything else to it. So we take the easy route and never go after God's perfect plan for our lives. It's like passing on a filet mignon and settling for Spam.

Out of Control

God doesn't start your stalled car for you;
but he comes and sits with you in the snowbank.
Robert F. Capon

Have you ever watched a child waiting around for his mother or father to fix something?

"Here, let me do it!" the child will say. The parent knows the child can't fix it, but after a five-minute chant of "I can do it! Let me do it! Gimme it!" the parent will sometimes give in and let the child learn a valuable life lesson the hard way.

What's the lesson? Despite what we think, sometimes we can't fix it. We may know exactly what we're going to do, but when we get the chance to do it, we often will discover that our plans simply don't work. The item (toy, bicycle, broken heart) is still broken, despite all our good intentions.

When we find ourselves in the middle of a major life crisis and we think we have all the answers, we get tempted to push against God's hands and plans and say, "Here, let me fix it!" God knows it's above us, but sometimes (after we've continued to insist on doing it our way), he lets us give it a try. And more often than not, we fall flat on our face. And the broken places of our lives remain broken.

When we at long last admit that the circumstances are far beyond our control, that we can't fix them no matter how much we want to, that we can't make them better, that we should have left well enough alone, we let God do what he does best—restore us and our problem to wholeness. But that doesn't happen until we finally reach a place where we'll give him control.

There is much wisdom in the famous prayer "God, grant me the serenity to accept the things I cannot change, the courage to change the things I can, and the wisdom to know the difference." Some things even God doesn't change. At least not back to the way they were. What's happened has happened. You can't change the fact that someone's carelessness (or perhaps even your own) caused the death of a close friend of yours. You can't change your doctor's diagnosis or the fact that your teenage daughter has run away . . . again. There are plenty of crises in life that we simply cannot do much about. But we can lean on the one who is faithful 100 percent of the time, loving 100 percent of the time, and good 100 percent of the time to help us get through difficult places like these.

So quit grabbing your brokenness out of God's hands and insisting on fixing everything yourself. There are some things you just can't fix. Admit it. As painful as it is, sometimes we just have to accept the fact that it's happened, learn from it, and move on, knowing that God loves us and hurts when we hurt, too.

The Promised Land always lies on the other side of a wilderness.
Havelock Ellis

The Last Laugh

Always laugh when you get the chance.
It's the cheapest medication we know.
Martha and Phil

What makes you laugh? We hope this book has (but not our pictures on the back cover). We hope it has helped you find something to smile about, no matter how "cold" this place of life is that you're in.

We have both spent our careers trying to help others focus on the funny, not because we wake up each day with a snort and a chuckle (our spouses might have something to say about that and might wonder what we just dreamed about), but because we've discovered that a good laugh is better than any amount of bran. But you may be wondering, what makes a humorist laugh?

I (Martha) love witty sayings. I love funny words embroidered on pillows, inscripted on plaques, written on billboards, or printed on greeting cards. I love funny words. I love funny e-mails from friends. I also love cartoons. I love watching talented comedians. Ray Romano, Steve Martin, Jerry Seinfeld . . . far too many comedians to list here; they all make me laugh. I love funny movies where the humor takes me by surprise. And I especially love funny moments with friends. Those moments when someone does or says something unexpected that you laugh about at the moment and for years to come.

Cartoons make me (Phil) laugh. John McPherson's "Close to Home" is a favorite. John has illustrated a few of my books, and I love his warped sense of humor. Last Christmas he drew a classic of a lady hanging a banner on the wall by the Christmas tree. Her husband was reading on the couch nearby and, frustrated at his inactivity, she hurled a hammer at him and yelled, "Why can't you help out a little!" The banner she was hanging? "Peace on Earth."

I showed it to my wife while she was hanging wall decorations. I'm not sure why, but she didn't think it was all that funny.

My dog makes me laugh. Her idea of play always ends with the word *treat*. She cleverly lures me into the kitchen, wagging her tail and hopping around as if I'm completely clueless as to her motives. She brings me her dog dish when it's empty and looks at me crooked as if to say, "And you call yourself a Christian! How could you? Must I report you to the animal rights people?" She's like my children were when they were small and all tucked in bed. They kept asking for a drink, thinking I was not wise to their ways. I had them figured out. But for some reason I kept bringing drinks.

Some of the funniest things have happened to me while I've been speaking, and they are far funnier when they are unplanned. One night I was telling people how old my parents were when I was born. I said my mother gave birth to me in an old-folks' home. That my loving parents bought my diapers with their pension checks. That my father used to play peek-a-boo with me. That's how he had his first stroke. Yes, I told them, "My dad was forty!" Most people found this funny. Except for a lady in the front row. She stood to her feet and yelled, "Hey, wait a minute!" She was quite obviously pregnant. Guess how old she was? Yep. Forty. And she was quite proud of her youth.

One night while I spoke to about three hundred souls at a banquet, a lady began laughing and couldn't find the Stop button. Everyone in the room was turning to look at her, so I stopped talking and asked if she was okay and would she like some oxygen? She laughed all the harder. It was contagious. Turning to a waitress, I said, "The rest of us would like whatever she's having." That didn't help her stop, either. Afterward I had to meet her. She was about my mother's age, and I gave her a warm hug. She said, "I lost my husband to cancer six weeks ago. My son has cancer, too. I haven't laughed like this in years. How I thank God for the joy he gives."

That kind of drives the sourpuss right off our faces, doesn't it?

Her words remind us of the reason we can laugh despite all that's going on around us.

And what is the greatest reason in all the world to rejoice?

It's the fact that a holy God loves the likes of us so much that he would rather die than live without us.

I (Martha) have taken a gift of a beautiful smoked turkey and incinerated it.[1] I've nursed my own wounds longer than they needed to be nursed, and I have on occasion wished for different circumstances rather than "accepting the things I cannot change." I've faithfully promised myself to get more exercise, get more rest, organize my life, and umpteen other promises, only to sit at my computer working late night after night, not getting either the rest, the exercise, or even the order that I needed.

I (Phil) am the guy who smoked every cigarette butt I could find when I was twelve—even ones in hospital ashtrays! I slid hamsters down banisters and put peanut butter on a cat's

---

[1] I didn't realize it was already cooked.

whiskers. I'm the guy who has harbored bitterness in his heart, and anger and fear. I've lied. I've coveted. And that's before breakfast.

And yet, the one who spoke the stars into space loves us. The one who knows us at our worst has offered us forgiveness and grace through his Son Jesus Christ. There will never be a greater closing line than that, so we think we'll end here.

Life, like the refrigerator, offers us a lot of good. It can also offer us some smelly circumstances, too, especially if certain things are left unattended for too long. But the good news is this: the light is still there, whether we've opened the door or not. It hasn't moved. It's ready to shine into our pain and cast new light on all our frustrations. So the next time you reach for the fridge door, remember the light that will never go out. (And while you're at it, a little chocolate won't hurt, either.) Even when we shut the door, it's still there, waiting for us to reach for the door and see it shining through once again.

I'll tell you how the sun rose—one ribbon at a time.
Emily Dickinson

Looking for more great books to read?

You can find out what is new and exciting with previews, descriptions, and reviews by signing up for Bethany House newsletters at

www.bethanynewsletters.com

We will send you updates for as many authors or categories as you desire so you get only the information you really want.

Sign up today!

More Side-Splitting Fun From Martha Bolton!

Filled with Bolton's signature wit and insight, this collection of humorous essays explores the various pros (and cons) of middle age.

Cooking With Hot Flashes

In this hilarious book, Bolton pokes fun at life after forty with comical comebacks for almost everything you'll deal with when you're finally headed over that hill.

Didn't My Skin Used to Fit?

A thoughtful but entertaining encouragement to "live your life on purpose." You'll laugh out loud with Bolton as she points out the often overlooked hilarities of life.

Growing Your Own Turtleneck

Give your mind a break from the stresses of life and see the humor in the ordinary. Instead of letting your thoughts give you a headache, use Bolton's recipe—laugh.

I Think, Therefore I Have a Headache